Stacked Against The Odds

ANTHONY FISHER

Library of Congress Cataloging-in-Publication Data

Anthony Fisher
Stacked Against The Odds
Edited by: Driandonna Roland
Published by: Fisher Publishing

ISBN 978-0-9978074-0-0

Printed in the United States of America

Note: This book is intended only as a real life testimony of the life and times of Anthony Fisher. Readers are advised to consult a professional before making any changes in their life. The reader assumes all responsibility for the consequences of any actions taken based on the information presented in this book. The information in this book is based on the author's research and experience. Every attempt has been made to ensure that the information is accurate; however, the author cannot accept liability for any errors that may exist. The facts and theories about life are subject to interpretation, and the conclusions and recommendations presented here may not agree with other interpretations.

Acknowledgments

As I begin to reflect on my personal life journey, I am reminded of all of the obstacles and challenges I faced as a teenager, young man, and an adult to achieve success. Everyone has hurdles they must cross, but with determination and a positive outlook on life, anything is possible! I dedicate this book to YOU! It is for anyone who has a strong desire to win or pursue a dream, even if you are *stacked against the odds*. I am a living testimony that dreams do come true. With persistence, the proper mindset, and mentors in your life, you can and will succeed. It doesn't matter what career path you are pursuing, as long as you have the ability to dream, this book is for you!

I was taught at a very young age to always cherish friendships and relationships, and to show dignity and respect for others. These values played a significant role in who I am today. To this day, my values have not changed. One thing I learned along the way: If you treat people like you want to be treated, it returns to you one hundredfold.

I wish to dedicate this book to my best friend, loving wife, but most of all, my true love.

Cherica has shown me everlasting love and kindness throughout our marriage and nursing school, and assisted me with the completion of this book. Thank you sweetie for your dedication and belief in me. I appreciate your patience and understanding while we embarked on this new journey. You have displayed an incredible amount of perseverance, determination, and resilience; for that, I am indeed grateful.

Preface

"I, Anthony E. Fisher, having been appointed an officer in the U.S. Army of the United States, as indicated above in the grade of CW3, do solemnly swear (or affirm) that I will support and defend the Constitution of the United States against all enemies, foreign or domestic, that I will bear true faith and allegiance to the same; that I take this obligation freely, without any mental reservations or purpose of evasion; and that I will and faithfully discharge the duties of the office upon which I am about to enter; So help me God."

This is the code of every Officer in the U.S. Military; a code which brings much camaraderie, dedication, and purpose while defending the United States of America.

Introduction

This is a glimpse of my road to success; an overview into the culmination of my life experience. As you read this book in its entirety, my aim is that you would feel inspired knowing that your dreams and future endeavors are possible as well.

Flying the Apache AH64D was one of the most incredible yet rewarding experiences in my life. It taught me the importance of determination and believing in myself. There were many doubters, dream killers, and naysayers, but they were wrong. I accomplished my goal and eventually had to literally pinch my skin several times because I could not believe I was actually flying this aircraft! The power of the 701C turbine engines, the agility this helicopter possesses, and its awesome capabilities made it all the more exhilarating. Because I was a man of integrity and honesty, I was being trusted with so much power. This helicopter has one the most powerful weaponry systems in the world and because of someone's belief in me, I was able to sit in the cockpit as the Pilot in Command.

It also gave me a sense of accomplishment yet this was only the start of much more to come.

This is my fascinating journey to success. If a small-town country guy can achieve this level of success, so can YOU! You can live your dreams. Never let anyone discourage you from living your full potential. When things get tough, pull through.

What you are about to read are facts. Even if you do not plan to fly, reading this book will teach you the dynamics of perseverance. Let me tell you a little about myself. These are my humble beginnings. Although I was born in Atlantic City, New Jersey, and raised in Tampa, Florida, I lived most of my childhood experiences in Live Oak, Florida. I graduated from Robinson High School on June 6, 1986, and was off to Basic Training on June 18, 1986. I have always had a strong desire to join the Army, and most of all, fly the Apache helicopter.

I had the wish, hunger, and desire to fly this specific aircraft for so long. This desire came to fruition in 1996 while attending Flight School at Fort Rucker, Alabama.

Before moving forward in this book, there is one particular person I must mention. He taught me the purpose of determination and gave me an incredible sense of accomplishment in my life. His name is Mr. Ben Coarde. This man is full of integrity and kindness.

He educated me on the importance of hard work and persistence. Through his leadership and mentorship, I gained an enormous amount of knowledge pertaining to work ethic, and I continue to follow in his footsteps.

Ben is a retired Air Force veteran. He has a lovely wife and family who reside in North Tampa, Florida.

I would be remiss if I did not mention the two who brought life to me and granted me an opportunity of "Life, Liberty, and the Pursuit of Happiness." To my wonderful and loving parents, Nathaniel and Doris Fisher. They have a loving marriage in which they have been married 50-plus years.

I come from a family of three brothers and one sister. I was raised in a little town called Live Oak, Florida, and boy, was it LIVE! Our household was filled with entertainment on a daily basis. You would think a small-town house was quiet, but we had the house going like a record player. We had live chickens to care for, rosters to tend, turkeys to feed, and hunting dogs on our property.

We loved all our animals and took very good care of them. All of these animals had names, to say the least. We had two dogs, one called Redd and the other Fido. I didn't think much of them and was not particularly fond of them. In my opinion, I thought these dogs were mutts, but that did not stop my brothers from giving these dogs so much love. They cared for them as long as the day gave light. Our favorite of all the animals was our turkey named Tom. Tom had a massive chest and strutted as if he were a peacock, and as strange as this may sound, I think Tom thought he was a peacock! As time passed, and with five hungry children to feed, Tom had to be slaughtered. This was devastating to my siblings and me because we never imagined eating Tom for dinner especially after becoming so attached.

We had a loving childhood. I remember going to church listening to my father play his guitar and singing to the congregation. In fact, I remember standing in front of the church at the age of 7 and watching the people stare at me as I mumbled the lyrics from my mouth. I knew from that moment I could not hold a note, therefore, I made excuses to stay home when I knew it was my turn to sing in church. Since we lived on the farm, for entertainment purposes we made our very own dune buggies from scratch. It was these interactions with my hands that gave me the idea that I could literally do and become anything I dreamt.

I am an average person with common ideas and goals. However, my background was not so average. As a lad, I spent countless hours on the farm learning about agriculture, and it was there on the farm that my work ethic began. When I was 8 years old, I already knew how to drive a tractor, work in the tobacco fields, crop tobacco, chop sugarcane, and feed cows and pigs. My grandparents owned over 300 acres of land, and I learned the importance of hard work while participating on the farm with the rest of my family. My dad would always talk to his children and say things like, "Son, when you get older, promise me that you will never work like this." That resonated with me! To this day, I am forever grateful for my father's wisdom and foresight. My dad worked at a large petroleum company that constantly demanded his time and attention, which ultimately led to his resignation. I saw the struggle in my father's eyes, and I promised him that I would make him happy one day.

I was reared in a loving environment, yet I was very poor. In fact, I was so poor that when my family moved from a little place called Live Oak, Florida, to Tampa, Florida, I thought I was in heaven, so to speak. The allure of the city lights, the huge skyscrapers, and the fascination of seeing what life was all about outside of the "country" really fascinated me. To be perfectly honest, I didn't know I was poor until one day in school one of my friends said, "Tony, if you live in that particular neighborhood you are simply poor." It was that statement that made me want to change the direction of my life.

The great thing about living in America is, it really doesn't matter where you come from or what background you have. If you have a strong desire to accomplish something in life, your background, ethnicity, or religious beliefs are never a hindrance.

Contents

CHAPTER 1

Pursuing Your Dreams

"Today I will do what others won't, so tomorrow I can accomplish what others can't."—Jerry Rice

Would you believe I needed my parent's signature in order to join the Army because I was only 17 years of age? When I graduated from high school, I thought I was "grown," sort to speak. I left for Basic Training (BT) on June 6, 1986, destination: Fort Jackson, South Carolina. My mother could not stop crying. Her eyes told me that she did not want her boy, now man, to leave. This was evident by how difficult it was for the bird to leave the nest. She was saddened that her son was leaving the nest yet my dad anxiously waved goodbye. It was a bittersweet moment, because my dad was happy yet my mom was reluctant for her son's soon departure. I had two goals: to become the best of the best, and to make my parents proud.

As soon as I arrived to Fort Jackson, South Carolina, the drill instructors (DIs) started yelling and screaming from the top of their lungs. They barked so much that at the end it seemed they were only yelling to yell. The DIs looked and acted as if they had just came out of penitentiary. I thought they had lost their minds because I voluntarily joined the Army and was not drafted...why would you yell at someone who volunteered? This really puzzled me, yet I remained unperturbed and stood my ground even deeply rooted in the stems of their screams. I soon discovered all of the chaos was intended to weed out the weak and solidify the strong. As the saying goes, only the strong shall survive. If you were capable of enduring the physical and mental stress of BT, then you were fit to be a soldier in the Army.

The things I found most difficult were learning how to type memorandums and using the military jargon. In fact, I had no clue about military structure, abbreviation, or rank. Everything was completely new to me. The military environment was so new to me that it fascinated me even more about the journey. I was thrilled about the new environment, which motivated me immensely. I quickly maneuvered through the ranks and made the rank of Staff Sergeant within five years. I joined the honor (color) guard and began to participate with other soldiers in retirement ceremonies, National Anthems, and largescale events for three- and fourstar generals.

After year three in the military, I received orders to begin recruiting duty. This was a dream come true! I graduated from recruiting school and started telling others about the benefits of joining the military. Not sure how I finagled getting these types of orders, but it was such a blessing! The learning curb quadrupled! After graduating from recruiting school, I had the honored badge of being an Army Recruiter. Before you have any preconceived notions about recruiters (because I had my very own thoughts), I was truly honest to all my applicants, telling the recruits of all the pros and cons of the military. My recruitment assignment led me to Warner Robins, AFB. I thought, *Why in heaven's name would Uncle Sam place me near an Air Force Base to recruit for the Army?* Little did I know this would be the launch of my success. Everything God puts in front of you is there for an extremely good reason. I went to many places I had never heard of. I began my recruiting journey and went to small towns I never had been to such as Montezuma, Georgia, and Hawkinsville, Georgia. I was a Sergeant at the time, but I was given the responsibility of a senior NonCommissioned Officer. I had my own government car, credit card, and supplemental eating expense account. I had all benefits imaginable. Going to high schools and colleges was one of my highlights of each day. I began to speak with so many students concerning the benefits of the military that even family members wanted to join the Army. It was as if I was letting other minds know that they could accomplish what I had. I had an unyielding desire to help others rise from a poverty-stricken environment to something that was more satisfying. This was my mission and goal in life — to empower others.

I was selected to participate in high school functions, college campus gatherings, and local events to promote Uncle Sam. I even became acquainted with college students at Fort Valley State University. This gave me an opportunity to not only endorse the Army but also make friends along the way. I became acquainted with many, and I remember going to a particular family's house telling them about the benefits of their son joining the Army. After convincing his parents, he was ready to join... he was "sold" to the U.S. Army. Little did I know this kid had a full-fledged academic scholarship to Georgia State University (GSU). This student was so impressed with his future of joining the military that he decided to enlist. I am sure that he was extremely happy; happiness practically radiated from his cheek to cheek smile. I was happy for him as well. The next day, I thought about my actions, and I told him that he should not join the Army but instead go to GSU and make a difference in the world. He listened to my advice, went to college, and did not go to the Army. This not only made me feel good inside, but it launched my recruiting career.

Many people began to trust me because of my honesty. I actually had more recruits join because of my integrity concerning the Army. This launched my recruiting career to a whole new level, and I was selected as the recruiter of the year for my battalion. One thing I remembered as a recruiter is someone telling me that most recruiters would sell you lies to get their bonus. I emphatically did not want to be known as a liar or a person of no integrity. This set me apart from others and further boosted my career and put me on a fast track for success.

I had a small seed of hope in me that kept telling me that if I stayed true and honest, everything else would just fall into place. And so with the correct mindset and positive attitude, I advanced quicker than before.

After my tour of recruiting duty, my next Permanent Change of Station was to a little city outside of St. Louis, Missouri. I was stationed at Scott Air Force Base, Illinois, where my life literally changed for the best! I was known for my veracity and was respected among my peers. This led me to climb the ladder of success with ease. I was promoted rather quickly and advanced to Staff Sergeant within five years of service. My destination would change, and becoming a Warrant Officer was the next goal to achieve. While stationed at Scott Air Force Base, I worked directly for a three-star general named Lieutenant General Kenneth R. Wykle. I somehow just found myself working in one of the best places possible, to me at least. How I got the position is beyond me, but

I always believed the favor of God was on my life and it followed me as I journeyed through my path of success. When interviewed for this position, LTG Wykle asked me what I envisioned for myself within the next three years. I was most definitely not afraid of dreaming big, and so I quickly voiced my dreams to him. I immediately responded that I envisioned flying an Apache helicopter and defending America.

He was impressed with the interview, and he highly recommended me for the Army Flight School Program located at Fort Rucker, Alabama. While working at the United States Transportation Command, I routinely led our unit's Army Physical Training Program and helped many soldiers who had difficulties running and passing the PT test. I was recognized as the soldier of the quarter and the soldier of the year by LTG Wykle. I observed his professionalism and dedication to the United States Army. His leadership truly inspired me, and he was the epitome of success in my eyes. I worked long and hard in order to achieve my goals. This was only the beginning of my pursuit to becoming an Apache pilot. My next transition was to overcome obstacles in this quest to flying, and boy, was I ready!

UNITED STATES TRANSPORTATION COMMAND
SCOTT AIR FORCE BASE, ILLINOIS

MEMORANDUM TO WHOM IT MAY CONCERN   21 April 1995

FROM: USTRANSCOM/TCDC

SUBJECT: Recommendation for SSG Anthony E. Fisher,
          for Warrant Officer Rotary Wing Qualification Program

1. I highly recommend SSG Fisher be selected for the Warrant
Officer Rotary Wing Qualification Program.

2. On 21 Apr 95, I interviewed SSG Fisher concerning his
application for subject program and found him to be an excellent
candidate. During the interview, SSG Fisher displayed all the
personal characteristics needed to succeed in this program. He
is intelligent, mature, articulate, and highly motivated.
Further, he possesses impeccable military bearing.

3. SSG Fisher clearly has the potential to be an outstanding
aviator and will represent the Army well as an officer.

KENNETH R. WYKLE
Lieutenant General, U.S. Army
Deputy Commander in Chief

Key Insight

A small boy, born on a small farm, owns nothing. He doesn't get what he wants; he gets what he needs. He has a strong mind, and a strong will to live. The boy is told by his parents every day to succeed by all honest means necessary. He has a growth mindset, he claps during awards ceremonies at his school, he cheers even though he is clearly not the one winning. He is destined for a great life; he can see that, even though others cannot see it.

Another boy, in a big city, he gets anything he wants; his father is the owner of a big company and makes thousands a day. He has a weak mind and thinks everyone is going to give him everything. He thinks he has no obstacles. His parents tell him that he should succeed by any means possible. He has a fixed mindset; his heart is filled with jealousy and hatred toward the teachers in the case when he does not get an award. He does not clap, smile, or even move at the slightest hint of foreign success. The chances are that he will not succeed.

We are all born with and develop skills. These skills determine our thoughts and our actions as human beings. Our circumstances and mindset also affect the development of our skills.

Being stacked against the odds can be a good thing, as it makes you a better person, as long as you decide to persevere.

Now, I am not suggesting that a person who does not have any visible obstacles won't succeed; I am simply saying that circumstances and environment can determine which mindset you have. Knowing this can help you change your mindset to the one of a winner. The key to success at this point is to change your mindset, if you haven't already.

CHAPTER 2

I Can Do It

"The brave man is not he who does not feel afraid, but he who conquers that fear." —Nelson Mandela

Let me tell you about my first experience flying the TH67; this is also known as a Bell 206 Jet Ranger helicopter. This helicopter weights approximately 3,200 lbs and hold 91 gallons of fuel. It has an average speed of 120 mph. The distance it can fly is approximately 300 miles with 30 minutes fuel reserve. The Bell 206 can comfortably seat four passengers plus pilot. This particular helicopter has high-skid type landing gear. The onboard equipment consists of a VHF radio, FM Radio, GPS navigational equipment, and cargo hook.

Before actually flying this helicopter, we had classes on the aircraft design and specifications. Additionally, these classes taught us the importance of safety and how to determine discrepancies. If there were anything out of the ordinary on pre-flight, it had to be fixed or we had to locate another helicopter to fly.

Now it was time to meet my first instructor pilot, who would teach me everything I needed to know about the fundamentals of aviation. I was a little anxious and tense but determined all at the same time. My instructor walked up to me and to my surprise he was older than I expected. The instructor pilot was a Vietnam veteran, and I immediately thought, *This guy is too old to fly, let alone teach anyone how to fly.* Boy, was I wrong! This instructor pilot did not only maneuver this aircraft, but he also made it look so simple. He actually allowed one student to sit in the front seat of the cockpit while the other student sat in the rear seat watching. Of course, I sat in the rear seat the first day because I wanted to see how well the first student who was my stick buddy would hover the helicopter. The instructor brought the helicopter to about 100 feet in altitude and gave my colleague the controls. He began to drift all over the place. I glanced over at his face, and he looked as if he were sweating bullets! I began to giggle silently because I knew I would do much better once I was given the opportunity. The instructor wanted to see how well he could maneuver the helicopter on his first day in the cockpit. Therefore, he allowed him to hover without his help to show it takes skill and practice to fly a copter. Obviously, he could not hover to save his life and it was a disaster. This was one of those moments when you are reminded that underestimating someone is not a correct nor a polite thing to do.

The instructor pilot regained the controls of the helicopter and conducted a traffic pattern. He showed us the flight pattern, the altitude to fly, and the radio calls we should always make before landing the helicopter. He finally landed and we swapped seats. I was now in the front of the cockpit with the instructor pilot. It was now my turn to hover and fly the same traffic pattern. I thought it would be a piece of cake since I'd read book after book about the fundamental of flight. I wanted to impress the instructor with my competence and ability. I was confident I would do everything correctly and maneuver this helicopter with ease. The instructor gave me the controls at 100 feet in altitude and said, "Anthony, you have the controls," I responded by saying, "I have the controls," and that's when I started losing control. Everything was out of control, and I have no idea how I didn't crash the aircraft. I began to speak positive reinforcement to myself internally, but it was not working. I began to freak out and panic; my heartbeat was through the roof at this point. The helicopter began to drift all over the place. I was sweating profusely. I had a death grip on the cyclic, and no one could pry my hands away.

I literally had a close-hold grip as if I were squeezing the life out of the cyclic stick. I even remember reading about over controlling the helicopter and possibly flipping the skidded aircraft. Needless to say, I never giggled at my stick buddy again. In fact, I had to overcome this obstacle by telling myself, *I can do it, I can do it.* It might sound ridiculous now but wait until you start flight school or a new endeavor; I guarantee you will remember my story. Even if you are not going to flight school, you will have those moments when you feel like you can't go on. At the times when you feel sick of trying, tell yourself to keep going. Always remember you will pull through.

I was out of my comfort zone and I disliked not being in complete control. I realized in order to grow, one must become uncomfortable even if it makes you sweat!

Every day in flight school, we would fly for a total of three hours. I would take the initial hour and a half and my stick buddy would have the remainder. Keep in mind, we were told that after we had flown for 15 hours we would fly the helicopter as a "solo" flight without the instructor on board. I did the math rather quickly, which equated to my stick buddy and me flying this helicopter in less than 10 days without an instructor on board! Not only did I have to get my act together, but my buddy needed to learn as much as I did if we were going to fly "solo." We would have to prepare ourselves both mentally and physically in order to pull it off.

Our Solo Flight

You would not believe how fast one week approached. I noticed when you are working hard, or learning hard in my case, the day will feel significantly shorter. The instructor had now informed the both of us that we were now ready for our solo flight. I thought the instructor was nuts. I felt my heart begin to make its way to my throat. Neither my stick buddy nor I felt confident that we were actually ready to fly this helicopter without our instructor, but he emphatically insisted we were ready, so by golly we were ready.

What I failed to mention about the TH67 helicopter is its landing platform. There are skids underneath for its landing gear instead of wheels to land. In other words, it's harder to land a helicopter that has skids than the one with wheels. If one lands the helicopter on one skid, a possible dynamic rollover could exist and flip the helicopter over. This is caused by having the pivot point to exceed its critical angle thereby causing a rolling motion. Once the helicopter has started to roll, and its critical angle is exceeded, it's more than likely the helicopter will flip. So this information added stress for me because I most definitely did not want to die. The instructors over emphasized this point to every student because they did not want to see an accident, and neither did I. So I told myself again, *I can do it!*

By this time I had realized that confidence was essential if I wanted to accomplish my goal. I tried to give myself pep talks as mental preparation after I realized this. The instructor gave us our pep talk before he departed the helicopter and said that he would be in the Air Traffic Control tower if we needed him. I thought to myself, *Are you seriously going to leave us in this helicopter with only 10 hours of training?!* My pep talk effect and confidence from the excessive and tedious preparation were wearing off by the second. I simply did not feel ready. The pucker factor just increased as we closed the door of this $1 million helicopter. Here we were, two newly assigned student pilots attempting to take off, fly a traffic pattern at 1,000 feet, and hopefully yet successfully land this helicopter without our instructor pilot at our side. At least we knew if he was there with us, he could simply take the controls and tell us what we did wrong. Now that he was not in the helicopter... we better have all of our ducks in a row! There was nobody to blame, which is the scenario that many people fear, in the subconscious levels at least.

Well, he allowed us to take the chance. Now it's no more giggling but all seriousness in the cockpit. We knew if we managed to blow it, we would go down with the million-dollar helicopter. I began to speak to my stick buddy with a calm angelic voice because he was first on the controls and I remembered how he previously flew. I not only wanted him to feel confident, but I also wanted to remain alive! I knew, at least for me, that staying confident was the only thing keeping me sane. I remember that on our base leg to final approach, I told him that we were still going 120 knots, and he needed to slow down. He said, "Roger," but his speed did not decrease. I knew we were traveling entirely too fast, and he needed to reduce this airspeed in order to land safely.

I began to speak more and told him to decrease his altitude and slow his speed. He again said, "Roger," but his adjustments were not fast enough for my comfort level. I began to feel as if I was powerless. I looked over at his face and saw that he was sweating profusely, so I didn't want to overwhelm him but I did want to stay alive. I saw him begin to freak out, and frankly I almost did as well. The only thing keeping me from screaming at the moment was the fact that I wanted to live to see another day.

We finally landed the aircraft, and I was the happiest man on earth. I was so happy to be on the ground that I almost kissed the ground when we landed. Now it was my turn to take the controls and fly this TH67, and his turn to call out airspeeds and altitudes. I understood why he had a monkey on his back, so to speak. When I took the controls to fly the helicopter, I had that same monkey on my back. I felt so much tension, stress, and butterflies in my stomach. I had to fly this helicopter and most importantly land. Taking off was the easy part! I feel that when you take off, there isn't much to it. All I had to do was gently pull up on the collective and wait for the skids to get light. Once I felt the helicopter lifting off the ground, I had to continue to pull upward on the collective and push the cyclic forward; thus we would begin to fly. Like I said, that was the easy part. Now that we had established 1,000 feet in altitude and flying at least 120 knots, the trick was to descend in altitude, decrease your airspeed, and land safely. Everything felt so surreal and for a few seconds I even felt disoriented. I remember vividly griping that cyclic with a kung fu grip! I even remember this calm, angelic voice talking to me (my stick buddy) telling me to "slow down and reduce your altitude, Anthony." Not only was he my stick buddy but a cheerleader as well in the cockpit. We finally landed the helicopter, and I knew that my stick buddy was the happiest man on the earth as well. Now we had both shared the pressures of both relying on someone for dear life, and being relied on.

Team Concept

My stick buddy and I learned a valuable lesson once we finished flying. Things were different and also difficult because we were used to training and practicing. I learned then and there the key to proper and good work ethic was to be able to work both alone and together whenever necessary in order to achieve your goal. We absolutely needed each other! We had all the necessary experience and knowledge to fly this helicopter but until our instructor pilot allowed us to fly solo, everything else was irrelevant. We did it! What we desperately needed was a big confidence boost, and once we helped each other through our first solo flight, our confidence levels shot through the roof! In fact, in life, you will always need someone to help, coach, or mentor you throughout your life's journey. I believe that everyone should have a strong mentor in their lives to keep them on the right path. I believe that one cannot be successful without being a team player or having that mentor in their life; as the saying goes, there is no I in TEAM.

Key Insight

Belief in yourself is one of the key factors to success. Ever heard of "Keep your eyes on the prize"? Imagining what it would be like is the key to figuring out how to get there. If you create that hunger to achieve, you will motivate yourself based on what is at the other end. Even if you are told by someone else that your goals are unrealistic or that you simply can't do it, know that you can. The person who focuses on what he wants and needs will get it. It is imperative, however, to not become overconfident; if you become overconfident, you will begin to underestimate others.

It can be pesky to have others telling you that you cannot do something. They are not able to see that you are a strong and mostly independent person, and so they will try to discourage you. They think they are looking out for you and usually do not mean harm. Do not gain resentment against those naysayers, instead build on their criticism and show them that you can do whatever it is you want to do.

If for some reason people are still telling you that you cannot achieve your goals, stay clear of those people. The people who still doubt you will try to bring you down. Get away from them as soon as possible. They will eventually get you to start doubting yourself. It is much better to be alone than in bad company. My recommendation is this: Renew your mind and stay away from negative people, thoughts, and surroundings.

After you have left these doubters, your motivation will increase and your health will improve. Stress coming from both working hard to achieve your goal and the naysayers will bring your health down and your will as well. Once you surround yourself with positivity, you will experience a big change in mood and will become more positive as the days pass.

If for some reason you do not feel more motivated, keep this in mind: You weren't conceived to live a life without meaning. You can do it!

Also, do not forget that you may yourself be a naysayer. If you do not think that you are a naysayer, keep your words under surveillance. We tend to only listen to what others say. Sometimes it is hard to notice our own defects and tendencies, as we live with ourselves.

With this in mind you are to also be an encourager. Do you not appreciate the occasional pat on the back or "Good job"? Be the person who encourages others. Surround yourself with fellow goal seekers. If you do this, whatever good gesture you do will most likely be reciprocated. This way you become symbiotic and help one another. The point in this is to not only surround yourself with kinder people, but to be the kinder person.

These are all good suggestions, but do not stray from the main thought: "I can do it".

CHAPTER 3

Stacked Against the Odds

"Forget all the reasons why it won't work and believe the one reason why it will." —Author Unknown

Although thousands of candidates are desperately trying to be accepted into the flight program, only a select few are chosen. My vision was ever before me of being one of the chosen applicants. I took the Alternate Flight Aptitude Selection Test (AFAST) in 1991. I was more qualified (in my opinion) than many other applicants who had taken the test. Not only did I have passing scores, but my scores exceeded the AFAST expectations. To my disappointment, I was not selected on my initial application and this baffled me greatly. I felt this was unjust and also unreasonable, but I do know that all things work together for the good. I could not understand how and why I was not chosen. After the denial letter, I continued to hope and dream of becoming an Apache pilot. Most people who experience this type of disappointment would fall into a state of depression, however, I kept my vision and goals ever before me because I knew that one day I would win. I kept standing tall and continued to imagine being selected as a nominee for the flight program. Although I was not selected on the first try, I did not give up. It was four years later that I resubmitted my application packet for the Aviation program, but this time, the letter stated, "Approved and Selected." Now that's what I wanted to hear!

Most people like a good challenge. In fact, we were made to challenge others; this is what makes us feel good about ourselves. We are living in a society where we are driven by being first place. We don't like losers; nobody does. Therefore, people aren't usually motivated because of self-betterment but because of being better than others in the sense that you have more money, or fame, or other things that don't truly matter. Case in point: Do you remember the name of the person who came in second place after Michael Phelps? How about the runnerup to Miss America? Trust me, we all love to win whether it's playing sports or simply winning a debate; it makes you feel good and it gives you a sense of accomplishment.

Winning, no matter how meaningless or null the game is, brings great satisfaction. We all like to win. We play games with family and friends and we want our victory. It doesn't matter if the game is against ourselves, i.e., solving a puzzle or playing Sudoku...we want to win. You simply finish the puzzle or Sudoku or you lose. This is where your outlook on life makes all the difference in the world. If one has a doom and gloom outlook, their future may be dull and dismal. If one has a victorious and successful outlook on life, then anything is possible to him who believes. If someone were to say to you, "Man, you can never become whatever it is you want to become/accomplish." What would be your response? Would you accept their derogatory advice or continue to believe in yourself?

Many people think that they wouldn't take the advice, but they would indeed take it. They would store it, think about it, and eventually lose willpower. It is extremely necessary to back away from people who serve no use to your life or goals. If you keep surrounding yourself with people who tell you no all the time, you will believe it. We live in a world where the truth isn't what is correct, but what the majority thinks is correct. It is better to integrate yourself into a community of like-minded individuals who will cheer you on and help you achieve your goal. That way, your dream becomes so believed in that it becomes true.

I personally knew several female Apache pilots who had all the odds stacked against them. They flew in a predominately male environment where they were belittled, ridiculed, and overlooked because of their gender. Many of the male pilots, in my opinion, did not think of it was appropriate for a woman to fly the Apache let alone become a pilot-in-command. I personally heard several disparaging comments like "She doesn't belong here" or "Who does she think she is." However, these same women prevailed over the insults, stereotypes, and derogatory statements. These women became strong and powerful beings who could no longer be deterred by either mental or physical means. In fact, these women went on and became instructor pilots or safety officers and continued to excel in many leadership roles not only in the United States Army but abroad.

I can personally relate because I experienced some of the same harassment but not to my detriment. Many of my close friends said that I would never become an Apache pilot. In fact, some laughed and mocked me when I shared my dreams and aspirations.]

When I initially joined the military, I was working as a clerk typist in an office environment. My military occupational specialty was 71Lima. At that particular time, it was not popular for a clerk to have aspirations of becoming a pilot. In fact, no one in my brigade had ever accomplished such a feat. I would often get mocked and ridiculed by my fellow co-workers. They made statements like, "Boy you better stop dreaming and wake up and smell the coffee!" "The chance of you flying an Apache are slim to none!" "Are you freaking kidding me, you better keep your day job." All of these statements from my so-called friends fueled my desire to win even more.

I happened to work in an aviation unit and my boss at the time was a UH-60 Blackhawk pilot. She was also called the Battalion S-1. She was given an opportunity to take her staff on a flight. We all boarded the helicopter and were excited for our first flight. While I was enjoying the flight, I imagined flying this aircraft. While the pilot was talking to Air Traffic Control, I began to imagine making radio calls from an Apache. I vividly imagined myself sitting in the cockpit making radio calls like my supervisor. This imagination sparked as we took off in the Blackhawk. After we landed the aircraft, I knew I was destined to become a fighter pilot and would not stop until it happened. After the flight, I learned a valuable lesson: Never tell everyone your dreams because some people were born to be dream killers. If you have a desire to achieve anything in life, and you feel as if you're stacked against the odds, nothing is impossible to him or her who believes.

A very dangerous thing can consume your being if you allow it...and it is called "failure." Let that sink in for a minute. Failure, as it is called by many people, is most definitely not a bad thing if one has the proper mindset. A failure, in my opinion, is simply a "hold" until things are perfectly lined up for your good. Imagine your path to success as a trip to the top of a mountain. When you "fail" you might accidentally find a cave or ramp to get to the top of the mountain faster. Do not set yourself up for failures though.

Given all the hardships I was dealt, one would think I didn't have a chance to attain any amount of success. My background didn't have anything to do with my accomplishment. It was my desire. I believe if adversity challenges someone, it gives the individual a greater sense of accomplishment. Fighting against any insurmountable odds makes you develop quicker.

I am definitely not suggesting that one must be poor or underprivileged to enjoy the finer things in life. I am proposing that if one is underprivileged, it makes him appreciate the things that are acquired. Adversity comes to us all — it is like time. Time is either on your side or working against you. It all depends on your perception. Do you either have a glass half full or a glass half empty?

One of the dichotomies of being an Army Officer is the frequent use of acronyms. In the military there are acronyms for everything! We are inundated with jargon, acronyms, and abbreviations. I will use my very own acronym of T.I.M.E. I glance at the word and my mind immediately thinks *Today I Must Educate* (TIME). If I sincerely want TIME to be my friend, then I must educate myself concerning my future, and I must respect time. Time is a powerful tool that can work both for you and against you. There can be time constraints, and there can be vacations and holidays. I believe that knowledge is powerful, but as Albert Einstein said, "Imagination is more powerful than knowledge." How do you see yourself in spite of adversity? Do you see yourself overcoming the many challenges you may face? When faced with difficulties, do you retreat or face your fear? Imagination can help you figure out how to deal with time and how to make yourself a better person. However you answered, just apply TIME to your situation and witness yourself overcoming these obstacles. Can you see yourself flying an Apache helicopter? Then just start to imagine yourself sitting in the cockpit making radio calls to the Air Traffic Control tower and ask for permission to depart the runway. You need to find yourself in the goal you plan to accomplish. Do you see yourself being a CEO of your company? Start to imagine having hundreds of employees working for your company completing one mission. How about envisioning writing a book? You need to imagine everyone wanting to read about your life story. These are only a few ideas you need to picture if you are stacked against the odds.

Key Insight

Imagine facing a warrior, 9-foot-tall monster of a man, with a menacing reputation and master of psychological and physical warfare. If you are not familiar with David and Goliath, let me briefly describe this event. David, who was a shepherd boy, was underestimated by all. He was in charge of taking care of sheep, while his brothers served on the front lines of the battlefield. He wore loose and light clothes, sandals, and maybe had a shepherd's staff and a sling shot. His assets were not visible nor was he qualified to fight such a giant. What he had was heart, fearlessness, and the knowledge that God was on his side.

When David heard of the devastating remarks being made by Goliath concerning his God, it provoked him to wrath. The stage was set; a physical giant would take on a spiritual giant — which would be the most outlandish confrontation in history.

———◆◆◆◆◆———

David was a great warrior and is an excellent example of someone who was stacked against the odds. He chose to face his giant with confidence and positivity. He never listened to negative talk. He moved away from his fears. He was open to hear from the one person who was on his side. He decided to do something about his situation without hesitation. Shortly, he accomplished what others said he couldn't. The truth is, like David, we all face insurmountable battles in our lives, our faith being one of them. We can retreat or imitate what David did and achieve the seemingly impossible!

CHAPTER 4

Adversity Is Good

"A man can fail many times but is never a failure until he begins to blame someone else." —John Burroughs

In the introduction, I mentioned I graduated from Robinson High School. While I was in high school, I had a strong desire to make the wrestling team. Unfortunately, I knew very little about wrestling — let alone any techniques or wrestling moves — but I did have a passionate desire for wrestling. I constantly envisioned myself on the mats wrestling with my fellow wrestlers.

I tried out for the team and was accepted to the 155-lb weight class. Since I knew very little about the event, I would watch and study wrestlers from other schools. I picked up on everything I watched and observed as if it were a lecture at a university. I would even stay after school to practice with the senior wrestlers since it was my first year and I wanted self improvement. I even purchased the movie *Vision Quest* to keep me motivated on my wrestling career. I constantly watched, heard, and looked for things that kept my motivation for wrestling fresh. I wanted to be the best and I believed that I could be the best. We would have "wrestle offs," which consisted of two guys sparring off in the same weight class. If you lost the wrestle off, you were automatically placed on the junior varsity team. I had no problems winning the wrestle offs. In fact, I was so confident in my abilities that I would challenge anyone on my team for a match. My efforts began to pay off and I eventually won against most athletes in my class, if not all. All this was driven by a spark that at a moment's notice became a wildfire. There were always one or two on the team who would give me a good challenge, but I could still defeat them.

My adrenaline started to rush whenever there was a challenge, because I was sure that if I didn't win, I could get better and truly become the best. I felt ready for the competition. Not only did this strengthen my confidence, but it gave me that boost that I needed when wrestling another team.

When I was ready for a wrestling match and the coach was behind me 100%, he placed me on the varsity team for my first match. The coach was aware that I was not only in it for wrestling, but for self-improvement as well. Our rivalry school arrived and my mind began to play tricks on me. I went to the mat with confidence, but when I got in the circle my mind started saying negative things to me. My mind told me, *Tony, you don't know this guy, and you definitely don't know his moves, how are you going to beat him? Look at him; he looks like he will demolish you, why are you going to embarrass yourself?* These thoughts would not go away! Guess what? I lost my wrestling match. I was pulverized by my opponent and even pinned to the mat! I went back to my wrestling coach and asked him to put me on junior varsity. He said, "No way, Tony. You are varsity material and you can win if you try."

The next week we had another wrestle off at my school with my teammates, and I beat them once again. Now it's time to prove that I am supposed to be on the varsity team. Once again I was out of my comfort zone. I didn't quite enjoy leaving my comfort zone, however my aim was to become better.

We were now at another wrestling event with a different school, and our team was doing well. It was my turn to step into the circle, and that old voice was coming to my head again*: Tony, here you go again, you know you don't know this guy either nor his moves. How do you expect to win?* I desperately tried not to listen to that voice, but I lost yet another match. I was 0–2. After the match, I told the coach to keep me on junior varsity until I felt I was ready for these seniors. The coach agreed, however, he really didn't want me to wrestle junior varsity since I had so much potential. This was precisely my adversity at that given time. Little did I know that my adversity would turn around for my good.

Since I was on the junior varsity team and this was by choice, the pressure was not as prevalent. I did everything within my power to improve myself. I ran between five and six miles every day consistently. I even talked to myself while running and convinced myself that I was a winner and not a loser.

Through confidence I made all my positive thoughts regarding my abilities true and exceptional. I told myself that I didn't have to know my opponent's moves, I only needed to pin my opponent. After a few weeks, I wrestled on junior varsity and it was like wrestling eighth graders. I won every match and begin to taunt the youngsters because I knew I was so much better than the junior varsity wrestler. I began to regain confidence and my comfort zone was leaving me alone in the glory of my accomplishments. After my third junior varsity wrestling match, I told the coach that I needed to be back on the varsity wrestling team. He agreed but insisted I complete another wrestle off with my teammates for formality. He already knew I would win but to be fair to the other wrestlers, we had to have a wrestle off.

I was back on the varsity team and was energized, fired up, and ready to defeat my opponent. I was so psyched; now I was using the same tactics my opponents used to deter me. I began to gain more and more confidence. I taunted the opponents by demonstrating my robust agility with the jump rope. This brought additional fear to the rival. This time, when I walked into the circle on the wrestling mat, I didn't hear that crazy voice any longer. In fact, my inner voice was telling me, *Tony, let's pin him to the mat within 30 seconds.*

Guess what? I did it. Not only did I pin him, but I pinned everyone I wrestled except one or two but still defeated them. I began to experience the rewards of making myself better. I worked so hard to push the cart up the hill and now for the fun part. I had so much fun wrestling that I went to the state championship my first year. The coach made me the captain of the team my second year. I tried so hard that within two years I was among the best, if not the best. I began to gain more confidence, even more than usual. I made sure to not get a big head about it though. At the end of the school year, I was recognized for the most improved, having the most pins, fastest pins, and most takedowns during the year. I received so many trophies that I actually felt bad for some of my teammates. I asked the coach if it would be okay to give a few of the awards to my teammates for their hard work. He agreed, and it heightened our team to another level. Our wrestling team became so great between my high school years, we began to have more people at a wrestling match than a football game. TV channels were out watching the sporting events and we were making progress in Tampa. Before graduating from high school, I was offered a full scholarship for wrestling to Iowa State, but declined because of my longterm goal of becoming a pilot. I played numerous sports in school, but I preferred wrestling over many other sports. Wrestling was the only sport in high school where it was just you and your opponent. In wrestling, you had no one to blame but yourself if you lost, and that's what I loved about it. What I learned the most is to never give up and keep a positive mindset to win.

I began to realize if I wanted to become the best at wrestling and managed to do so within only two years, I could literally accomplish anything. Only then did I realize that wrestling was both my debut at reaching goals and my practice run.

Key Insight

Changing your mindset is pivotal, and this was previously covered in Chapter 1. Being an open-minded individual can make you a desirable employee, or employer if you like. What sets apart the closed-minded individual from the open-minded individual is that an open-minded individual has the desire to learn and advance in life.

There are two main mindsets in the human consciousness: people with a fixed mindset and people with a growth mindset. People with a growth mindset tend to use an obstacle to their advantage (e.g., It is raining so we cannot go have a picnic, but we can collect the water to refresh everyone and we will have the picnic tomorrow). In a fixed mindset, the person just throws their hands in the air and waits until the obstacle is moved by someone else.

It is important to have a growth mindset, because in reality, Big obstacles are good. Big obstacles help build character, help you learn, and make you appreciate the easier moments in life. Without night, day would be meaningless. Without water, land would be useless. We need to accept the fact if we want something good, we can either endure the bad for a little while and have happiness for the rest of our life, or be happy for a little while and suffer for the rest of our lives. Trust me, having the correct mindset can help you pass tests, overcome challenges, and allow you to radiate positive energy for others to access. Even if you feel that you have missed some important moments while trying to accomplish your goals, know that it will be worth every hardship when you finally achieve your dreams. With that being said, if something's meant to help you in pursuing your personal growth, it will wait for you and you will walk in confidence when pursuing your dream.

CHAPTER 5

Living Your Dreams

"When you cease to dream, you cease to live."
—Malcolm S. Forbes

How do you start living your dreams? Well, start off by having a vivid imagination of what you want to achieve. Living your dreams is more than a figment of your imagination; it is a reality if you choose it. You should become so fascinated about your future that you begin to have dreams; everything you think about is relevant to you becoming that reality. When you begin to like what you are dreaming, you begin to analyze how to get there. By the time you begin to assess how you will get to your goal, you are already on your way without knowing it. Once you become obsessed with your dreams and start to think of your success, the stars will begin to align in your favor. It literally has a self-fulfilling prophecy. When you believe what you say and feel the emotions after speaking your dreams, your subconscious starts believing it also.

Everything you say will then start to align and all of your actions will begin to work in your favor. Imagine becoming anything you want in life… that's one of the most fascinating gifts about our imagination. No one can place a hold on your imagination and the stars are literally the limit.

Go ahead, start fantasizing of being this pilot, CEO, entrepreneur, or whatever you chose to accomplish in your life and watch what happens. Just work as hard as you can, only looking back for inspiration and truth. Everything will fall into place if you stay true to yourself and your goals. Sometimes what you start out with isn't what you end up with. You might start trying to become a manager of a store and end up being a CEO.

One Small Step Closer to Flying an Apache

The imagination of flying the Apache came to reality, but I had to first believe that it was possible. Every day when I woke up, when I ate, when I worked out, and when I went to bed, I imagined myself being that Apache driver. This dream came into fruition when I was accepted into flight school and started my journey through the aviation process. Before strapping in the cockpit, you had to learn the basic aerodynamics of the aircraft, the fundamentals of flight, and important concepts concerning the dynamics of drag and other elements. This is a crucial component of aviation, because it greatly reduces the efficiency of any helicopter. Hard work had to be done as well, but it is well worth it when you have the end result in your mind. After weeks of learning the fundamental principles of flying in the classroom, it was time to put knowledge into practice. As mentioned earlier, the instructor pilot ensured we could successfully fly one of the basic helicopters before moving to an advanced aircraft. If students could prove their competence in the Training Helicopter (TH67), we were advanced to yet another aircraft. We slowly but surely advanced up the stepping stones to success. We were now moving to Phase II in flight school where we learned instruments, warfighting skills, and maneuverability.

Learning how to fly another aircraft took hours and hours of study, yet the mechanics of flying were the same. All helicopters have the same basic controls to maneuver, which are the collective, cyclic, and pedals. There are panels, buttons, and toggle switches one must master to safely take off, descend in altitude, and most importantly land the aircraft. Once these switches are committed to memory, it reduces the stresses of flying. Helicopter pilots must know every inch of the controls in the aircraft to feel completely secure while flying because you must always be prepared for an emergency. However, if you were born with the innate ability of dexterity and could easily control three moving parts simultaneously (collective, cyclic, and pedals) while making radio calls to the Air Traffic Control tower, monitoring other flying helicopters, and changing radio frequencies constantly, then flying would be a piece of cake. But what is a little elbow grease when you know that end result will be much better than the beginning? The difficulty with flying a helicopter is that no one seemed to be born with that intrinsic ability to automatically multitask. This took months and months of practice, and eventually the novice pilot became the expert and was eventually placed in a more advanced helicopter. The fortunate part about aviation is, unless you were a bigheaded genius baby, the playing fields were leveled.

The next step was learning how to fly the Bell OH58 Kiowa Observation Helicopter. This particular helicopter has been in the U.S. Army's inventory since 1969 and was used in the Vietnam War Era. It is currently used for scouting and has been retrofitted for reconnaissance. This aircraft is more advanced than the TH67, yet there are similarities. One of the differences with the TH67 and the OH58 is the amount of power it possesses. The TH67 has only 420 shaft horsepower whereas the OH58 has a total of 650 Shaft Horsepower at the pilot's discretion.

In Phase II, we were introduced to more advanced skills like autorotation and stalls. As soon as we left the basics and began to work on complicated tasks, the interest and curiosity were at their highest. If you were to study the concept of autorotation, it would fascinate you. To grasp the concept of an actual autorotation, imagine flying a helicopter and your engine stops performing while flying 6,000 feet in altitude. What do you think would happen? Would the helicopter just fall out of the sky? Nope. Thanks to autorotation, the pilots could disengage the freewheeling unit and allow air to move through the rotor system from below as the helicopter descends. This incredible concept gives the pilot, in an emergency condition, the ability to safely land the helicopter. Once the aircraft reaches an acceptable altitude, preferably just above the ground, the pilot adjusts the collective stick to carefully land on the terrain. To be perfectly honest, it didn't matter how many books I read on the concept of autorotation, when the instructor pilot simulated shutting off the engine while we were in flight, the pucker factor shot through the roof again. I panicked. The initial feeling was, *We were going to die*! In all actuality, I was a novice pilot and did not know what to expect. I became nervous at performing flights with my instructors when it came to autorotations. The phenomenon was baffling, helpful, and scary at the same time. In retrospect, now as a senior combat aviator with over 1,800 hours of flying time, I think the concept of autorotations are entertaining and humorous. It makes me appreciate my humble beginnings during flight school.

I relate this autorotation experience with living your dreams because you may have bumps and unexpected turns during your pathway called life, but keep the vision and dreams in your forefront and ride life to the fullest. Through your trials, try to enjoy whatever life throws at you, even when it feels like you are going through extreme turbulence. When it feels like you are falling from the sky, remember the autorotation and how to safely land.

Autorotation gives you the idea that even when you feel you are beginning to fall, you can simply use the conditions to your favor. You can make the most out of any circumstance and progress in life. Don't worry; just enjoy the ride and watch how you safely land. If it is night time, go to sleep and rest for tomorrow, or get a flashlight and get back to work. It is all up to you in the long run.

Once completing Phase II, the next and most important step was preparing for advanced placement of aircraft selection. This was one of the most critical and life-changing events in my aviation career. Based on your standings in class, your grades, and your abilities to maneuver the previous helicopters, you were given the choice to fly either the Blackhawk, Kiowa, Chinook, or Apache helicopter. I was hoping that my test scores and flight abilities with the previous helicopter would give me an edge for selection of the AH64D Attack Helicopter. With the grace of God and favor from the instructor pilots, I was assigned to fly the aircraft of my choice. I don't want to sound biased because all the helicopters are excellent to fly. However, if you want to feel the excitement or if you are an adrenaline junkie, you need to fly the Apache! Maybe the idea of demolishing targets from 6,000 meters away excites you, or you have a fascination with shooting hellfire missiles, rockets, or large 30mm bullets; then you definitely need to fly the AH64D.

The Apache has the capability of carrying a variety of munitions to include hellfire missiles, rockets, and 30mm rounds. I can describe in details the capabilities, but you will not quite understand until you sit in the cockpit and feel the power and thrust of this multimillion dollar aircraft. Since you decided to pick up this book, I will assume that your desire to become anything you place in your mind will come to pass. I just happened to choose to become an Apache pilot.

First Day in an Apache Cockpit

I made it to the most important part of flight school, so let's talk about the first day in an Apache cockpit. My adrenaline is really kicking right about now! First of all, you must understand that there are two different types of Apaches. The AH64A is an older type and model, but the characteristics are the same. This helicopter has been transitioned from the regular Army to most Army National Guards and Army Reserves units.

Next, you have an AH64D. This is what you will fly at Fort Rucker, Alabama. This helicopter is equipped with all the latest technology to include the most updated software, radios, and navigational equipment. Most of the AH64A model aircraft do not have the most advanced technology. However, it is still an Apache helicopter, and it is still a beast to fly.

The very first day was nothing like I thought it would be. The instructor pilots were top-notch trainers, ready and willing to see you succeed. They ensured you knew what you were doing and if you had a question or didn't know the material, they taught you. The instructor pilots treated you with respect and wanted every student to pass their check rides and advance to the next level. They were very encouraging and reassuring.

One of the most challenging times during the first week in the cockpit was the "bag" phase. This phase of training is vital because the instructors are ensuring you fly the aircraft solely on instrumentation. This is critically important, especially if a pilot becomes involved with Inadvertent Intermediate Meteorological Conditions. The pilot must trust the instruments with no reference points outside the aircraft without exception.

You have got to be kidding me right!

During this phase of training, black curtains are placed throughout the cockpit allowing the pilot to only utilize those instruments in the aircraft. The curtains made it impossible to look outside the aircraft for a reference point, and this is scary for the novice pilot. This eventually makes an average pilot into a stellar pilot. With no contact with the "outside" you begin to actually fly this aircraft using your instruments. It will seem and feel a bit awkward initially, but I promise this technique is intended for your personal development and prowess as an Attack Helicopter pilot. For those of you who are already instrument rated, this might seem easy, but for those who never sat in a cockpit let alone flew instruments, it can be challenging. It really tested both your patience, sanity, and skills. May I be perfectly honest with you? My brain did not want to accept the fact that I was sitting in an aircraft and was not able to see outside due to the curtains. Not only was it dark in the cockpit, but I felt a little claustrophobic.

Here is the analogy so that you can appreciate what the novice pilot had to endure. Imagine driving your car with black curtains around every window and driving on the interstate with bumpertobumper traffic. How would you feel if you were in a blacked-out motor vehicle with the exact same scenario? This is exactly what I experienced. In the classroom environment, the teachers emphatically taught us to always trust our instruments. You never know when you might unexpectedly fly into the clouds and need that black curtain experience. It is important to know everything, no matter how pointless it may seem.

You must realize the Apache is unlike all other helicopters, in that the pilots are in an individual cockpit and unable to see each other. Unlike the Blackhawk, Chinook, and Kiowa where the pilots are seated next to one another, in the Apache helicopter, the pilot and copilot have tandem seats.

The first day, you will fly in the copilot gunner seat, or what is called the "front seat." You will learn the basic skills necessary such as making proper radio calls, repositioning the aircraft from the parking area to the actual runway, and hovering using different symbology. Once you have mastered these techniques, you will be ready for more advanced training like gunnery and shooting rockets and 30mm guns. This is probably the most exciting part of your training, so prepare to have fun!

It is now time for gunnery. Although everything is in a canned scenario, who cares… you are getting ready to fire ammunition down range, right? You are now ready to disintegrate all targets, after all this is what you've come to flight school for, right? The instructor pilot tells the armament personnel to load 38 rockets and 600 rounds of ammunition. You are sitting in the front seat feeling the adrenaline rushing through your fingertips. Ready to squeeze the trigger at a moment's notice, you are feeling a bit antsy. The instructor pilot makes it to the firing range and tells you to "match and shoot." You lob your first rocket down range. You see the explosion of the rockets, and this gets you even more excited. He tells you to match and shoot again, and you feel the power and force that is expelled from this powerful piece of machinery. You are now ready to fire the powerful 30mm gun. There is a soft target that is 2,100 meters away. He says, "Fire at will." You place the gun setting on burst of 30 and anticipate the rounds hitting on impact.

Let me explain the importance of an HE round in the AH-64. The M230 is mounted on a chin turret that allows the gun to rotate in various angles. It uses a 2-horsepower electric motor to fire 30mm link-less ammunition at a rate of 625 (±25) rounds per minute. Although that is a lot of fire power, most pilots set the rate of fire to about 300 rounds per minute with a 10-minute cooling period as the gun is air cooled. The gun was made to endure the harshest environments. Due to the rapid rate of fire, it was specifically designed to prevent jamming and open bolt clearing. Extra casings are ejected overboard through the bottom of the gun where the rounds fall freely to the ground.

The mount on the AH-64 uses secondary hydraulics to move the gun. Elevation is provided via a single hydraulic actuator located on the gun's centerline just forward of the pivot point. The gun is spring-loaded to return to its centerline stowed position with the barrel angled up about 11 degrees in the event of a loss of hydraulic power. This allows the gun, which is mounted below the copilot station, to collapse cleanly into its designed space between the pilot stations in the event of a hard landing. This prevents the gun from entering the pilot's station and becoming a hazard.

The Apache is capable of carrying up to 1,200 rounds but because of the internal fuel tank, it reduces the capability to 300 rounds. This is still very effective against any enemy due to other firing capability of the helicopter. The ammunition is loaded into the AH-64D Longbow Apache by armament personnel using an aircraft-mounted motorized loader and special ammunition handling tray.

The M789 HEDP is the primary tactical round of the Apache AH-64 helicopter, widely used in current combat operations. The Apache's ability to provide accurate air support with minimal collateral damage led to increased use and volume demands for M789 ammunition.

The M789 is typically used in the M230. Each round contains explosive charge sealed in a shaped-charge liner. The liner collapses into an armor-piercing jet of metal that is capable of penetrating more than 2 inches armour. Additionally, the shell is also designed to fragment upon impact, which gives the HE round in the Apache an unfair advantage in combat. The 30mm bullet takes about 4 seconds to travel 1,000 meters (or 3,300 feet). However, as the shell slows down, it takes nearly 20 seconds for it to fly 3,000 meters (9,800 feet). Now that you have a better understanding of one of the armament on the platform, you can appreciate the cause of this intense adrenaline. The realization that you are actually firing live rounds from an Apache platform did not "set in," but you pinch yourself because this is a dream come true.

Can you imagine yourself in a scenario such as that? Then let's make it happen! Daily envision yourself becoming whatever you set your mind to. Tell yourself that you can do it and nobody can stop you. Don't let anyone steal your dreams; you have the power and desire to fulfill your destiny.

Key Insight

One of the most repeated set of words on the face of the earth is to "Believe in yourself." Believing in yourself is very important and also has a great part in you succeeding in anything. Believing in yourself is not always easy but you can start by renewing your mind. Get rid of self-doubt, don't dismiss compliments nor criticism... there is a need for both.

Belief is also connected to purpose. Your purpose has been decided before conception, eons ago. Many of us aren't aware of our potential until we start living our destiny with purpose. Once you find your purpose, walk in it and pursue it will all of your being. Many people who are not in the correct mindset can be envious of those who are near the fulfillment of their own. Do not let others keep you from fulfilling your goals.

You must be willing to go far for your destiny. If you wish to achieve something momentous, do not hesitate to go to great lengths to accomplish it. Stay the course, and remain focused! Before long, you will have succeeded beyond your wildest dreams. Now dream big!

CHAPTER 6

Mr. Know It All

"Pride goeth before destruction, and an haughty spirit before a fall." —Proverbs 16:18

Once training was complete at Fort Rucker in the Apache helicopter, I received orders to my first duty assignment at Camp Humphreys, South Korea. Talk about an experience! I arrived to my new unit, B Troop, 3rd Squadron, 6th Cavalry Brigade, wide eyed and bushy tailed! I was ready to start my new journey and I knew I would be flying with the best of the best aviators. Because I was "fresh" out of aviation school, my company commander paired me with an experienced Aviation Safety Officer.

Let me be the first to give anyone some advice. When arriving to your first duty station, you are considered the most junior officer. Although you completed flight school, you are considered the least smart coupled with the least experience, so shut up and learn. In other words, don't be a Mr. Know It All! It would behoove you to find a senior officer who will take you under his wing and show you the ropes. Look for someone who is very experienced and apt to teach. If you do this, you will not only set yourself up for success, but you will stand out as one who is seeking to improve his technical and tactical prowess. It is important to not ever become complacent. Your familiarity with the aircraft makes you the expert in your field, however, never lose respect for its power and maneuverability.

Mr. Know It All has always been disliked among fellow comrades. Although there will always be one or two in the crowd, don't allow it to become part of your life. In short, close your mouth and open your ears; that way you know what you are doing wrong and what you are doing right. Don't become a Mr. Know It All...it makes people dislike you anyway, and it makes you a person to avoid in terms of job and growth opportunities.

It is important to live up to the expectations of the people you work with, regardless of the rank structure. It is imperative to learn the necessary skills to improve your tactical proficiency. Since I was one of the new aviators, I was told to avoid or never correct my instructor pilots because they are the experts. I felt uncomfortable at first because I wanted to show forth my book knowledge, but it was futile. Book knowledge and experience are two separate entities.

A brand-new aviator from flight school is a "newbie" and needs to be trained to standard. Therefore, you will train in different stages for your progression. You will be assigned as a Flight Activity Category (FAC) level 1, Readiness Level Three (RL3) aviator. I'll explain these terms later in the chapter. Your goal at this point is to show your proficiency so that you can progress from RL3 to an RL1 pilot.

The requirements are easy to meet: Simply do what's asked and study. You must show proficiency and maintain a fundamental knowledge of the skills that were taught in flight school, to include navigating, radio calls, hovering, etc. Once you pass from RL3, you are elevated to RL2 status. This mean you are safe to fly with another pilot besides an instructor pilot. You have met all qualifications, and the instructors are confident in your abilities to maneuver, execute, and safely fly the aircraft. Although you will be proud of your accomplishments of attaining RL2 status, you are not quite ready to fly on your own.

You must achieve RL1 status. This is significant because once you achieve RL1 status, you are considered combat ready and capable for war. In each phase, you are given 90 days to accomplish the entire task.

Most young pilots finish their RL3 to RL1 status within 90 days unless weather or maintenance does not allow. You will be fine and should progress as normal, but the key is to remain focused and always arrive early for preflights, and know your chapters 5 and 9…these two chapters are instrumental in Army aviation.

As a pilot, preparedness is what sets you a part from others. Therefore, it is important to work hard and study hard. Studying will make you knowledgeable in the sense a little extra knowledge might be the difference between life and death. The basic knowledge of chapter 5 and chapter 9 of the AH64-D helicopter manual, also known as the dash 10, are non-negotiables. Meaning, when you arrive you better know these chapters without exception! If you have a clear understanding of these chapters, you are already ahead of the game.

As previously stated, once you are RL1, you are released to fly with other aviators. This is a very invigorating feeling — something that is almost indescribable. Once I was released to RL1, my trainer happened to be a seasoned safety officer with lots of experience. He was known as one of the best pilots in the company. I will call him John Doe for the sake of anonymity. This guy was the most laid-back but confident aviator I had ever met. He could maneuver this helicopter like a remote control! His precision, accuracy, and technical expertise could not be matched by any other. He happened to be an Aviation Safety Officer as well. He knew his stuff. He was an avid Harley Davidson rider, hunter, fisher, and a great outdoors man. We had a lot in common and we bonded rather quickly. He could relate to my experiences on the farm and understood the complications of a new aviator. He showed compassion and strength during our flights. He was known to lead the battalion from the front and always had a delicate spot for new aviators.

We were scheduled to fly on a routine training mission (ATM training) day out and night return in the lower parts of Camp Humphreys, Korea. Things were going great. John asked me if I wanted to practice landing and taking off, and of course I agreed. First, he would demonstrate how to land the aircraft properly in the dirt, gravel, and uneven terrain. He made certain the helicopter was approaching the termination point at an airspeed that was no faster than a brisk walk. After we had landed the aircraft, he asked me if I was ready for the next approach. We did the transfer of the controls, and I took off with a left base to land to our termination point. As I was nearing my approach angle, I started my descent. CW3 Doe stated that my airspeed was much too fast especially for a junior guy, so he demonstrated the technique again. We did a few more landing and departures and at that point, I was comfortable with the maneuvers.

The night was fast approaching, so I asked if we could do one last approach before we departed the area of operations. His response was, "Sure." We conducted our before-takeoff check, cleared the airspace left, right, and overhead, and immediately took off for our final landing.

While I was very close to the termination point, I fixed my eyes on that termination point. While my eyes were fixed on the point of landing, I drastically decreased my approach path inadvertently to the point that the helicopter flew into wires. I could not believe what had just happened! CW3 Doe yelled, "Pull up, pull up!" and he immediately took the controls to land the helicopter safely.

CW3 Doe told me that our helicopter had struck wires, and we needed to land the aircraft. At this point, it was as if life were moving in slow motion because I saw every spark from the wire strike. Sparks were flying everywhere, and as I looked outside the cockpit, I noticed neighborhood lights were being shut down due to the wire strike. At this point, I knew that I had really screwed up. I thought for sure that my career was over. We actually got out of the aircraft to check for damage and I could not believe what I saw. There was NO DAMAGE from the wire strike. Due to the Wire Strike Protection System (WSPS) that is located near the wheels of the aircraft, it literally sheared the electrical wires, thus causing the sparks. I was angry and upset because I couldn't manage to take control of the aircraft. I felt embarrassed and shameful, but the experienced pilot reassured me it could have happened to the best. We called for the safety team to arrive and inspect the helicopter before flying back to our base camp.

Not only was I angry for flying into the wires but I was also freezing because it was the month of December. It was one of the coldest nights in Korea and since we didn't anticipate having an accident we didn't bring extra cold weather clothes. We actually slept in the cockpit with the Auxiliary Power Unit running to minimize freezing. Before we landed the aircraft, we radioed our distress and waited patiently for the UH60 Blackhawk to arrive. Flight operations launched a Down Aviation Recovery Team helicopter to fly us back to Camp Humphreys. Unfortunately, the inclement weather prevented the UH60 from rescuing two stranded pilots and they had to Return to Base until weather permitted. We actually slept in the cockpit and had to Remain Over Night due to bad weather. This gave me all night to think about my actions and what could I have done differently to prevent this mishap.

The following morning, the weather finally cleared and we made another radio call to give the exact location for the incoming aircraft. The UH60 spotted our aircraft from a distance and began to start its approach to the intended landing area. Once the Blackhawk landed and the blades finally stopped rotating, my heart really started to pound. I didn't realize that an entire entourage from my unit would fly out with the DART aircraft. On board the aircraft were the Battalion Commander, the Flight Surgeon, the Battalion Safety Officer, the Brigade Safety Officer, and all of the DART personnel. I thought to myself, *Oh boy, you really did it now.* What I didn't realize was the surrounding city had already telephoned my Battalion Commander and given indepth details of damages and possible cost the government should pay the citizens for their misfortune. Whenever any branch of military is utilizing another country's resources, we pay a hefty price if any incident occurs. Trust me when I tell you the South Koreans were very familiar with the intricate details of making the government pay.

We finally made it back to our unit, and we had to undergo standard operating procedures to ascertain no drugs or alcohol were involved in the incident. We painstakingly endured all of the "red tape" to ensure we met all proper protocol. We were literally escorted to the military hospital for blood work. This is better known as going to the hospital to "piss and bleed." We gave urine and blood samples to the flight surgeon. He could verify that neither one of the aviators was under the influence of any type of medications or drugs. These were the standard operating procedures for aviation mishaps during my tour of duty in South Korea back in 1998, and I certainly guarantee things did not change when it involves a mishap.

One thing I failed to mention: After an aviator has an accident he is automatically reverted to RL3 status and must prove to an instructor pilot he is capable of being an RL1 aviator once again. Because I recently made RL1 status, my check ride would be with an external instructor pilot who was unbiased concerning the incident. Unfortunately, all of the blame went towards CW3 Doe because he was the Pilot-In-Command (PIC). Once an aviator earns the impressive title of PIC, he is solely responsible for the outcome of that particular aircraft regardless. After this mishap I was more careful and made sure to analyze and assess the situation carefully. I was embarrassed and ashamed of my actions for weeks. It was a valuable lesson learned that eventually caused me to become ever so familiar with the intricate details of flying. It also gave me a chance to embark on an additional career opportunity I not only wanted to be a Pilot in Command but also an Aviation Safety Officer. To this day, I am known for my meticulous attention to detail when it comes to mitigating risks.

Low-Level Flight Over Water Flight

The flights in Korea were interesting. One of the unit's missions was to fly over water and shoot Hellfire missiles. If you know nothing about the Hellfire missile, let me explain briefly its capabilities. The Hellfire missile is an air to surface (ASM) missile first developed for anti-armor use. It was later developed for precision strikes against other target types, and has been used in a number of targeted killings of high-profile individuals. It was originally developed under the name *Fire and Forget Missile*, which led to the colloquial name "Hellfire" ultimately becoming the missile's formal name. It has multi-mission, multi-target precision-strike ability, and can be launched from multiple air, sea, and ground platforms, including the predator drone aircraft. The Hellfire missile is the primary 100-lb class air-to-ground precision weapon for the armed forces of the United States and many other nations. When I first fired this missile, it left an impression that would never be forgotten. The thunderous sound and devastation of the Hellfire missile can be seen and felt for miles.

Of all the training I received in Korea, this was probably by far the best. This type of training in and of itself was well worth being assigned to Korea. I thought to myself, *How many other junior aviators would be able to say they flew over the Yellow Sea flying at airspeeds of 170 knots and an altitude of 100 feet above the ocean?* Talk about a rush! While flying these incredible airspeeds, we collaborated with UH60 Blackhawks, which were overhead at 300 feet, and above the UH60 were the P3 Orion (fixed wing) aircraft directing the Apaches to fictitious targets to locate and destroy. While flying over water, aviators wore a Mustang suit. This suit is designed to keep the body warm in the unfortunate event an aircraft inadvertently goes into the ocean. This Mustang suit is worn over your flight suit and can get a bit uncomfortable. We also had special equipment for over water flying, such as heeds bottles and special gear. It was a little uncomfortable initially, nevertheless, it was required. The flights over the Yellow Sea were exhilarating, however most pilots are extremely exhausted from flying nearly nine hours in over water gear.

Key Insight

Sometimes people gain too much confidence. Becoming overconfident will lead to arrogance and ultimately being a Mr. Know It All. They rarely listen to others and view other opinions as a threat. They will use knowledge to put others down to feel superior. To avoid being a know-it-all person, stay humble and respect others. Humble people work hard and are always willing to learn from anyone. Learning is a big part of the human experience. In order to learn it is imperative that you stick with others who know more than you. We learn from our mistakes and successes alike. Remain humble so that you can be teachable, and one day you may be able to instruct others.

CHAPTER 7

Overcoming Obstacles

"The greater the obstacle, the more glory in overcoming it."
—Jean-Baptiste Poquelin

Along the way you will find that life is full of many challenges. To overcome these barriers, you must believe that you were created for a purpose. You were designed to overcome any difficulties or challenges that will constantly remind you of your frailty. There were a few people who helped me along the way to overcome the obstacles I faced. They were my mentors. Mentors build relationships and enhance lives. They are often experienced individuals who are willing to train and guide you to your greater good. In mentoring another, one does not need to be formally educated as you suppose. Instead, the mentor or coach must be knowledgeable. Knowledge is acquired from real-life experiences. Education and knowledge are distinctly different. Education is obtained through schooling, universities, or other formal institutions. Believe it or not, even a child can have more knowledge than an adult. Education has a system for learning whereas knowledge has no barriers.

While participating for the next Top Gun award, I needed to rely on my mentor. The stress levels were intense and my mentor provided feedback, clarity, and positivity, which helped me remain focused.

It was during a livefire exercise, and my goal was to become Top Gun pilot. We were scheduled for a live gunnery shoot at the MultiPurpose Range Complex (MPRC) in South Korea. Here is where the rubber meets the road. Pilots are now ready to perform at their best! Each pilot must demonstrate his or her technical skills and proficiency. Your performance is under scrutiny because every pilot wants to be the next Top Gun. In all actuality, other pilots are watching your performance to see if they can beat your times and learn from your mistakes.

Each gunnery scenario has time constraints and the quicker the copilot and pilot respond to the target, the better the outcome. There were approximately 10 scenarios for each crew to engage, but I will only discuss a few. I can remember one of the scenarios so vividly because the stress levels were high. Both the pilot and copilot sit in the cockpit waiting for the targets to appear. The control tower would state, "Scan your area." Immediately, both pilots were instinctively in the attack mode searching for any moving targets down range. If one of the pilots saw the target first, he would say, "I have a moving target at 11 o'clock approximately 1,500 meters." The response of the copilot would hopefully sound like, "Roger, I have the target, preparing to engage with rockets." If all goes well, the scenario will take no longer than two minutes to scan, detect, and destroy.

The next scenario tests the pilot's ability to prioritize. The control tower states, "You have two moving targets, scan your area." Now it is of vital importance for the pilots to not only communicate effectively but to differentiate which target is the priority. The pressure is now intensifying! The key is to remain calm, listen to the inner voice within, and know you GOT THIS! All eyes are watching and hoping that you make a mistake because only one crew will earn the prestigious Top Gun award, and remember you have eight more scenarios remaining.

Before an aviator can experience such scenarios, he must pass the Helicopter Gunnery Skills Test prior to firing on the range. This test consists of basic questions concerning the 30mm ammunition, 2.75 FFAR rocket, and Hellfire missile. The test is given by the Master Gunner, who is a seasoned Apache pilot. Upon completion of the test, results are computed for the final score. Your test score and MPRC results will determine which pilots are considered Top Gun. Once results are posted, the crew will officially have bragging rights for being the best pilots for that year!

Key Insight

Mentors are highly important and are crucial in the human development. Everyone has had a mentor in their life one way or another. Even musicians, athletes, political leaders, or the average person has mentors. Let's look at Lebron James, Michael Jordan, and the now retired Kobe Bryant. These men did not reach their level of success alone. What they all had in common were coaches, teachers, and someone to help guide their career along the way. Maybe these people found comfort in trying to go above what they were raised in.

The point is, a seed won't grow on its own, and mother earth cannot on her own host life. Everyone has had a mentor. My first mentor was my father: He was a firmly believing Christian with wholesome values that he instilled in me since birth. I respected my first mentor and always have, will, and still see him as a man with integrity and values.

My father was a mentor to me at all times and continues to be. We would talk and interchange ideas and feelings when we went fishing or hunting. It wasn't to catch fish or hunt, but to bond and understand each other. The mentor who was solely responsible for me obtaining the Top Gun award is my father. I reflected on many of our previous conversations about why it was important for me to succeed. My dad is a loving man who instilled greatness in me, and I am forever thankful. To this day, I have always respected him and held him in high regard. Without him actually being in the cockpit, he provided insight on ways to maintain a positive attitude and never give up. My father was never formally educated; however, he has a wealth of knowledge. When faced with stress or difficulties, I would reminisce on my childhood experiences and overcome those challenges.

The second mentor is Mr. Ben Coarde. I met this phenomenal man while dating his daughter in high school. He is a man of generosity and courage. He did not want any scumbag dating his daughter. He watched me intently before giving his stamp of approval. Mr. Coarde and I developed such a meaningful relationship that he eventually trusted me with his daughter. Many people tended to flock toward him because of his straightforward personality. He is very bold when expressing himself, which led others to want to emulate him. I especially was drawn to him because of his military service. I knew that one day I would join the military, and because of his mentorship it became possible. He began to share with me some of his experience while serving in the Air Force. I looked forward to listening to his captivating stories, and little did he know this would catapult me to become a successful Army Aviation Officer. Even though my relationship with his daughter did not matriculate to marriage, today Mr. Coarde still has an everlasting impact on my life.

One of my greatest mentors in my life is certainly a giant in my book. He left a lasting impression that changed everything about me. Lieutenant General Kenneth R. Wykle is a leader's leader. He commanded thousands of airmen, soldiers, sailors, and Marines while performing duties as the Deputy Commander in Chief, Scott Air Force Base, Illinois. This base serves as a Joint Transportation Command. While working under his leadership, I observed his daily routines. He consistently demonstrated leadership at a higher level. He spoke with great confidence. Although he had great military rank, he showed such dignity and grace for all mankind. No one felt unimportant in his presence, and there I learned the meaning of how to treat others regardless of their socioeconomic background, rank, status, or position in life. While admiring him, I wanted to exude the same professionalism and confidence he displayed. Today, he is still my mentor and I remain in contact with him.

Now that you have completed this chapter, reflect. Think long and hard about all the mentors who made an impact on your life.

CHAPTER 8

Military Moves

"To improve is to change; to be perfect is to change often" —Winston Churchill

If you knew how many times my family and I relocated due to military orders, you would probably think we were vagabonds! These numbers might be alarming if you are not well-versed with military relocations. We moved a total of 14 times in 23 years...talk about feeling like the Beverly Hillbillies! The moves became so frequent, we instinctively kept some of our belongings unpacked in the attic. We moved to Germany; Kentucky; South Carolina; Savannah, Georgia; Fort Hood, Texas; South Korea; Fort Polk, Louisiana; Fort Rucker, Alabama; Fort Bragg, North Carolina; Phoenix, Arizona; Scott Air

Force Base, Illinois; Warner Robins, Georgia; Clarksville, Tennessee; and Belleville, Illinois; just to name a few of the locations. It was difficult for our children to ever have any stability in their schools due to the constant moving.

I enjoyed most of my transitions; however, my children did not always relish being uprooted from so many schools. My kids had to make new friends and meet new classmates and teachers, which was a frightening experience. This was the expected life of the Army Officer... and as the saying goes, it comes with the territory. After my tour in Korea, I received orders to Hunter Army Airfield, which is located in the beautiful and historic city of Savannah. I thought to myself, *It doesn't get any better than this!* Of all the places we had traveled in the United States, Hunter Army Airfield seemed to be the most favored. Who would have ever imagined that I would be living my dreams and receiving the ideal duty location? As most realtors say, "Location, location, location." Savannah was the perfect opportunity to enjoy the beaches, historic downtown area (to include the famous St. Patrick's Day festivities), and so much more. While stationed at Hunter Army Airfield, our unit was one of the first to transition to the "newer" helicopter. All the pilots in our unit had to receive additional training in order to fly this AH64D Longbow.

All Apache pilots had to report to Fort Rucker for temporary duty for additional training in the new and improved Apache Longbow. Once we arrived to Fort

Rucker, the instructor pilots notified our unit that the training would be held in Phoenix,. Everyone was happy because it meant an all-expense paid trip by the government to Arizona and possibly a tour to the Grand Canyon. Yes! I was so excited about this upcoming tour. Since this was my first trip to the Grand Canyon, I was even more motivated. The trip was great, and before we actually started with the academic environment, we were given a tour of the Boeing Plant where the helicopters are manufactured. It was quite fascinating to see how this multimillion dollar helicopter was built from scratch. You will not believe the technology and complicated bundles of wiring that are ran throughout the helicopter. Every inch of the helicopter was filled with hidden fiber optics which were carefully designed and mapped together. The weight of this helicopter alone makes it unfathomable to fly. The total weight of an Apache is nearly 16,700 lbs. With the advanced rotor system and turbine engines of 1,870 Shaft Horse Power, these engines lifted this horse like a feather. The average cost of the AH-64D was nearly $24 million, and I took pride flying this stealthy beast.

Once the tour was over, we started our academics and began to fly this new and improved helicopter. When we strapped in the cockpit, it was as if we were playing a computerized game. All the old instrumentation was no longer there. All new software, to include touch pad computers, was installed in the cockpit. We had two monitors that looked identical to a miniature laptop in the aircraft. This was the latest and greatest technology. Everything was at a push of a button. It made flying so easy. In fact, there is a device on the cyclic called hover hold and one called altitude hold. Once these buttons are engaged, pilots could literally fly the helicopter with hands off the controls. It was like flying on cruise control. While on tour at the Boeing plant in Arizona, we actually worked Monday through Friday and weekends were free, so guess what we did on the weekends? You guessed right, we took our weekend trip to the Grand Canyon and had a blast. Since that was my first visit to the canyon, I took lots of pictures and walked until I was completely exhausted. If you have never visited the Grand Canyon, make it one of your tours in the future. You will be glad you went.

Our battalion had to fly cross country from Arizona to Georgia in our new helicopters. We managed to log many hours of flight time. The flight was like none other. We stopped at various locations to refuel our aircraft, and everywhere we landed, we felt like celebrities from Hollywood. After hours of flying, we finally made it to our designated location (Savannah). Our return trip to Savannah was a great experience. We were motivated more than ever because we had completed our training; therefore most of us felt like we were on top of our game.

While transitioning to my new unit in Savannah, I was surprised how my reputation preceded my arrival. When I initially reported to my unit, I heard other pilots say, "So you are Anthony Fisher." I greeted them kindly and immediately asked, "When can I start flying?" I was still motivated and eager to get in the cockpit although I had only been flying the aircraft for one year. One thing for sure, if other aviators see how enthusiastic and eager you are to learn, you would not believe the amount of flight time you can accumulate. I tried to fly on every flight possible because I wanted the experience and I additionally loved to be in the cockpit. I even volunteered for all static displays and test flights.

A static display is when you fly the helicopter to either a park or some special career day so civilians can mount the aircraft and ask questions concerning the helicopter. It was more of a recruitment technique that gave civilians an opportunity to see the real Apache helicopter up close and personal. I assisted in lots of maintenance test flights whenever possible; this gave me an edge on learning the helicopter from many of the test pilots as well. The more you are in the cockpit, the better prepared you are as an aviator. This eventually will have you prepared in a time of war or when an emergency arises.

Little did I know that my knowledge and expertise in this aircraft would lead me to fight in combat during Operation Iraqi Freedom (OIF III) from 2005 to 2006. Our unit received orders to Iraq and was destined to depart within 12 months. The unit had to undergo rigorous training before deploying to Iraq. Preparations are the key to any successful mission. Our unit deployed to Fort Polk, where we trained intensively for war. This training was realistic both day and night. The training provided necessary tools for the success of our unit in the upcoming war. We were being watched and graded on every task from start to finish. Our unit had the opportunity to train with new and improved technology known as the Longbow Apache helicopter.

Our mission at Fort Polk was to provide security for each convoy that departed the Forward Operating Base and interdict any alleged insurgent activity. Once we completed this training we departed to Fort Bragg and made final preparations for our unit's deployment.

Each day prior to deployment was cherished. Due to the yearlong departure, our company commander attempted to give as many days off to compensate for the upcoming days missed with our families. In fact, when our unit was less than 90 days from departing for Iraq, commanders ensured families spent quality time together. The company commanders understood the hardship of yearlong deployments and how they can adversely affect any military family. Family support groups (FSGs) were established to keep the wives or husbands busy while their loved ones were away fighting a war. Family support groups also played an instrumental role in the morale and support of many soldiers. These support groups would send care packages and volunteer their time to aid and assist other families that were enduring a hardship. The FSG had lots of structure and coordination to support the deployed soldiers. Many of the wives volunteered their time and finances to help in mailing care packages and to build a strong support group while the spouse was away fighting a war. Most gatherings for the FSG took place at the company commander's house, and this is where most updates were discussed among the spouses.

Key Insight

Planned or unexpected moves can cause strain on military families. It is important to have family support groups in place. These groups provide moral support during times of deployments and offer a variety of counseling services. While I was deployed to Iraq, the Family Readiness Group always provided care packages and kept my family informed concerning my wellness. This made my deployment less strenuous knowing we had this as an added benefit.

Life can take us by surprise! Planned or unexpected moves can shake the best of us. Some people have support groups to depend upon, while others don't. When faced with uncertainty, one can learn how to manage change, embrace fears, and adjust attitude to improve their circumstances. Remember, life is not about what happens to you, but how you react to it!

CHAPTER 9

Fly like an Eagle

"One can never consent to creep when one feels an impulse to soar." —Helen Keller

Now it's time to fly like an eagle. The eagle flies alone at high altitudes. Never will you find an eagle mixing with other birds. You heard the saying "Birds of a feather flock together." Well, no other bird goes to the height the eagle does. Eagles cruise at altitudes at which only they can cruise. Eagles naturally have strong vision. They have the innate ability to focus on their prey up to five kilometers away. It is imperative to keep the vision in front of you and remain focused while pursuing your goals. Like the eagle, we were created to be independent and free. We are here to use our abilities for the greater good.

Iraq Deployment

Our deployment to Iraq was like none other; it took our battalion nearly 19 hours to fly overseas, which was one of the longest flights ever. We departed to Kuwait on a jumbo 757 to our final destination in Camp Taji, Iraq. Camp Taji is located approximately 17 miles north of Baghdad.

It was time to say goodbye to our families and loved ones. It was especially hard because of the possibility of never returning home. All of the families knew our battalion would not return for at least a year, and the thought of the yearlong departure made it even more difficult. Before departing on the airplane, families were crying and children were hugging their father's legs trying not to let them go. It was indeed a very heartbreaking moment, but we were called for the mission.

After the 19hour flight, we finally made it to Kuwait. We were in Kuwait for 30 days to become acclimated to the extreme heat of 125+ degrees Fahrenheit. Needless to say, dehydration and heat exhaustion were a constant concern for the battalion and company commanders. Most soldiers were not prepared for the intense heat. Our company suffered from heat exhaustion, heat cramps, and heat strokes. Mandatory formations were enforced in order to instruct the younger soldiers to hydrate, which mitigated the chances of a heat casualty.

The entire experience in Kuwait was physically and mentally demanding. While there, we had scheduled test flights and continuous missions to simulate battle in Iraq. Unfortunately, our battalion lost one of the pilots in a routine training exercise. The pilot lost control of the helicopter and plunged into the desert floor, killing the copilot gunner. This devastated our battalion and soldiers mourned greatly for their platoon leader.

Once we arrived to Camp Taji, Iraq, mortar attacks from the enemy occurred daily. Soldiers had to shelter themselves in concrete bunkers to stay alive. Camp Taji was bombarded with mortars consistently and after several months of being attacked by mortar rounds, most soldiers took the mortar attacks lightly. By the ninth month of mortar attacks, many soldiers did not even run to bunkers or shelters. We always knew when new soldiers arrived in the country; they would "haul ass" to the concrete shelters while the senior soldiers casually walked to safety.

While in the bunkers we jokingly laughed at the newbies because we were now counting our days to go home!

Aircraft ShootDown (Fallen Angel)

One night, I had an indepth conversation with another pilot. We literally talked and laughed for hours on the night before his flight. He said, "FISH, I can't wait to go home on vacation." I asked him why he was so anxious to get home. He informed me that his wife was pregnant, and he was excited about their first born. I told him congratulations on the upcoming birth of his first child and told him that his wife would be glad to see him. We reminisced about the good times with our families and discussed our vacation plans once we arrived home. Unfortunately, my friend's plans with the family never came to fruition. Within the next 24 hours, we lost two pilots due to a shoot down by a surface to air missile. The pilot never got a chance to see his wife nor his newborn.

One of the toughest lessons any soldier has to endure is watching his friend lose his life from an aircraft shoot-down. This is very debilitating. Infuriated by the loss of our two comrades, pilots strapped in the Apaches searching for the cowardly insurgents. At that point, our battalion commander called an emergency briefing to all the pilots, informing each of us to maintain control of our emotions. He said that we are here on a mission to provide air support and security for our ground troops not for revenge! He said other choice words and everyone knew that he was upset about the loss as well. We had to maintain our focus and remember that this was our call of duty because there was no turning back. At this point it became clear that everything came at a cost. This great nation has been maintained by the brave men and women who work hard in order to ensure our freedom. We mourned internally and comforted one another.

Although pilots were cognizant of all of the AK47 small arms fire and rocketpropelled grenade shots being fired at the helicopters, it really didn't seem to bother us until we encountered our very first downed aircraft. I can vividly recall one of our night flights with night vision goggles when my copilot witnessed hundreds of rounds being fired throughout the sky at our helicopters. After witnessing such things, I realized that even with all the preparation in the world, the only way to get over the death of someone isn't to get over it but to put that person to rest. We had to experience these sort of things in order to truly know that the United States of America was brought up on hard work and dedication, with many sacrifices. I am proud to say, however, that today we do not only defend mother liberty, but also democracy and humanity.

While flying on a day mission, we both teasingly stated it's better to fly the day missions, because at least we didn't see tracer rounds during daylight operations. This gave us a false sense of protection because the insurgents were trying to shoot the helicopter down during daylight operations as well as night time operations… we just could not see the bullets. The insurgents had a mindset to destroy all Americans, but if they could bring down another AH64D, it would be a great accomplishment for them.

Every day Improvised Explosive Devices (IEDs) exploded, killing an unsuspecting convoy. The rules of engagement had to change! Any insurgent found digging holes at night would be eliminated…no questions asked! Every precaution had to be taken in order to avoid any more casualties. Sometimes one terrorist had to be eliminated in order to keep thousands alive. After all of the IEDs and bombing that occurred, something different had to take place.

With advanced technology, the insurgents would use cell phones to detonate bombs on small convoys. Some of the terrorists literally got away with murder. This was one of those moments when technology was not for us but against us. The most frustrating of all missions is to watch one of the Humvees get struck by these bombs and see how it could sever the vehicle and destroy everyone inside. IEDs were being placed on primary roads; convoys began to take secondary (dirt) roads to get to their designated targets. Unfortunately, the terrorists had learned of the new routes that soldiers were taking to get to their locations.

Convoys were bombarded by these devastating bombs daily. Ground forces were reluctant to leave the Forward Operating Base without having air support on deck. Soldiers began to become paranoid as these detonations became quite common. One of the most difficult missions was to provide security for convoys. Under intense pressure, pilots had to look meticulously for any possible IEDs then warn the convoy commander of imminent threats. I had personally witnessed numerous deadly detonations of IEDs on friendly personnel. One Humvee was hit, and the aftermath was devastating. These IEDs would completely destroy a Humvee and everyone inside.

Our camaraderie for each other grew stronger as the constant barrage of mortar attacks, IEDs explosions, and suicide bombings continued daily. We became a close-knit family that cared for each other and made sure to tell each other what was on our minds. We always made sure to trust each other. I constantly reminisce on the radio call to assist our ground forces. Two Apaches were flying in the vicinity of Baghdad International Airport when we received the call from our Brigade Tactical Operations Center (TOC). I can vividly describe and recall that moment because it seems like yesterday. The company commander (Death Stalker 06) and I (Death Stalker 08) were called to assist our distressed American ground forces. Our soldiers were taking over-whelming fire from three cells of terrorists and desperately needed additional fire support.

The call from our TOC sounded something similar to this: "Death Stalker 06 and Death Stalker 08 we have ground forces needing immediate support from terrorist cells... State your location." Once we gave our location, we were told to expedite our airspeed and immediately assist with the small arms fire attack. We hightailed to rescue our ground forces. The American ground troops were elated when Apaches were on scene to assist with their overall mission. We saw men that hoped to see another day of their hardworking lives. They looked exhausted and scared at the same time.

Once we arrived on the scene, the ground forces gave a quick situation report of three cells of insurgents suppressing and decimating their bunkers. Death Stalker 06 was lead aircraft and we were wingman (Death Stalker 08). Our Apache came in strong and fast with speeds ranging from 160 to 180 knots and at an altitude of 50 feet or less. The speed and height prevented any insurgent from placing our aircrafts in their crosshairs while flying. The shock and awe of the helicopters made the terrorist run like cowards! One of the things the terrorists feared most was the incredible firepower of an Apache! Speed and agility of the aircraft brought massive fright to the terrorist cells. Once on scene, the American forces gave the specific locations of these three terrorist cells. Bloodsucking insurgents were infiltrating the Americans. Bullets were literally flying everywhere when we arrived on scene.

The American forces would constantly state on the radio, "Death Stalkers your aircrafts are taking fire from three cells of insurgents at the 3 o'clock and 12 o'clock position." While flying, the rebels shot at our helicopters with AK47s and rocket-propelled grenades. There were cells of insurgents located in a small shanty, another cell located in the tall bushy grass, and the last cell of insurgents located in a shallow ravine. We had to determine where these shots were coming from and find them before we had another aircraft shoot-down from the insurgents! We lobbed 30mm bullets, 2.75 rockets, and even Hellfire missiles to defeat the enemy. It was a successful mission, and we were not going to let another American die on our watch!

BDA Damage

After the firefight, we landed our aircraft to conduct a Battle Damage Assessment (BDA) at the Baghdad International Airport. BDA is the timely and accurate estimate of damage resulting from either a firefight or enemy shots. This can be either lethal or nonlethal, against an objective or target. To our amazement we counted 13 bullet holes throughout the entire helicopter. Our aircraft was shot 13 times by an AK47 and a possible RPG, but that did not stop our mission to assist these ground troops. Unbeknownst to our aircrew, insurgents were hiding in tall grassy areas waiting for our aircraft to fly over them. Every time we flew by the insurgents, they fired shots at our aircraft. These cells of insurgents were found and dealt with if you get my drift! We found it rewarding to aid and assist our comrades in the time of need. BDA includes physical and functional damage to the aircraft as target system assessment. Although producing BDA is primarily an intelligence responsibility, it requires extensive coordination with operational elements to be effective.

I immediately began to praise God and thank Him for the safety of our crews and for keeping HIS angels all around us! In that battle, we definitely flew like an eagle.

Key Insight

Flying brings great ease. It makes you free in the sense of bodily constraints. There are no limits but the ones you impose when you fly. When an eagle sees danger it will fly above where nothing can harm it. The eagle will gracefully maneuver in the sky, finding its target and avoiding its attacker. Eagles use their abilities to their advantage. The eagle uses his wings to rise and push himself against storms. The eagle is strong, courageous, and afraid of nothing. The eagle uses its grace and ability to overcome anything that comes its way. The eagle is independent. We can use the challenges of our lives as stepping stones to rise to greater heights like the eagle. We can soar!

CHAPTER 10

Defending America, the Real Price of Freedom

"He who would accomplish much must sacrifice much"
—James Allen

There is absolutely a price for freedom and someone had to pay the ultimate sacrifice. Soldiers sacrifice their homes, families, and quality of life to go and protect this country. Some returned with memories of the combat zone and battle scars as reminders; this is the real price of freedom.

Many do not comprehend the intricate details of a war zone, which is certainly understandable. Some are swayed, in my opinion, by war movies that are diluted with misconceptions of an actual combat zone. The war movies are not how real wars are won! The price of freedom is characterized by blood, sweat, bombs, fear, chaos, confusion, and much more. Before entering a war zone, there must be preparations to fight the enemy. Our unit prepared for an entire year for the combat mission in 2005. There were strategic plans that were developed, practiced, and executed prior to launching this military operation. These plans have contingencies due to the fluidity of the battlefield.

The countless hardships military personnel must undergo while in harm's way are relentless. From the colonial times, to now as the United States, we have stood the test of time to become one strong nation. It was not easy but sacrifices were made and now we are a world power. With those sacrifices, many lives were lost on the battlefield and soldiers have come and gone from war to war since 1774. I could mention numerous names of fallen comrades of Operation Desert Shield/ Desert Storm, Operation Iraqi Freedom, and Operation Enduring Freedom... they are the unsung heroes of war.

Readjusting to the normal way of living is a difficult task for some yet others continued to live and function as usual. Many returned as amputees while other had shattered limbs and traumatic brain injuries. The devastation of what is seen by soldiers and the emotional drainage it caused can leave an everlasting impact. To watch a suicide bomber walk into a mosque and kill everyone inside is unfathomable. The gruesomeness of an IED explosion leaves an undesirable impression that cannot be erased. It does not matter how much counseling one receives, the reality of war is repugnant. The frequent nightmares, anxieties, and insomnia that are caused in a war zone are the price we pay for freedom. PTSD, or post-traumatic stress disorder, is a psychiatric disorder that can occur following the experience of a life-threatening event such as military combat, terrorist incidents, or serious attacks. This traumatic stress can be caused within any branch of the service and not only in the Army.

PTSD was prevalent among returning personnel because of their experiences while in combat. The disastrous symptoms of PTSD may continue after soldiers arrive home. PTSD is a challenge many veterans have to endure. The war has a devastating effect on all family members. Some lost their families, jobs, and homes after returning from the war zone, which makes defending America even more challenging.

In my opinion, the Veteran Administration (VA) was not prepared for the influx of registrants, which led to the backlog of disability ratings. The devastation of amputees receiving only 20–30% disability rating from the government tells me there are tremendous flaws in the system. It breaks my heart to hear stories of veterans returning to the United States of America after fighting a war to become homeless. It breaks my heart to hear stories of combat veterans not receiving the proper coverage from the VA after fighting on the battlefield. Believe it or not, some soldiers have to fight nail and tooth to receive their rightful disability ratings.

After the deployment, it is even difficult for some to find employment. Although programs have been developed to help veterans in times of crisis, this is not enough. There is a desperate need for mental health counselors, registered nurses, and other medical personnel to assist veterans. Fortunately, some received counseling and therapy to cope with the many distresses that were faced while in the combat zone while others fell through the cracks.

As a nation, we are still dealing with the mental crisis of the war zone. The devastating impact of a war must not and should not be overlooked.

Since my transition from an Apache pilot to the nursing field, I distinctly remember caring for a combat veteran in the hospital. It was a clinical day and I happened to be a nursing student with my preceptor. According to the veteran's statement, he had a horrible experience during his hospital stay. He yelled and used vulgar language and profanity at the nursing staff. This tension created fear among the nurses. At one point, the nurse dreaded administering his medications. He was a veteran with PTSD and recently returned from war. Although the staff were highly trained, they had difficulties relating to his circumstances. The veteran stated that his nurse did not understand what he went through and she didn't believe he was in pain.

I established rapport with the veteran and soon discovered he was upset with his disability rating from the VA. He was so furious, he didn't want to speak to anyone who did not understand his plight. After I told him that I was a retired Apache helicopter pilot, we began to communicate on our experiences in the military. He and I reminisced over the times we shared in Iraq and actually talked about the good Army days. This conversation with him calmed his demeanor and helped him cope with his frustrations. He needed someone to listen to his real-world experiences. Before my shift was over, I suggested he visit the VA for counseling. He agreed. It was a 12-hour shift, and I devoted much of my time to this patient. Towards the end of the shift, I asked the veteran to be polite to the nursing staff and he obliged. That was one of the most rewarding clinical experiences as a student nurse; I just happened to be at the right place at the right time for the veteran.

Now that I am a registered nurse, it saddens my heart when I speak to patients who feel they are alone and have absolutely nobody to care for them. I often sit and just listen to their stories because most times they only want a lending ear. It can be both therapeutic for the listener and the speaker because they get to show their emotions without being criticized.

I frequently educate retirees, veterans, and wounded warriors of all of the benefits and resources available for them, and sometimes it seems as though it is not enough.

Homeward Bound

We finally received orders to depart from Camp Taji and return home. This was one of the greatest feelings one could have. After experiencing all the devastation that war came with, we felt both physically and mentally exhausted. Our year in Iraq had finally ended. After 12 to 14 months away from the family, it was now time to say goodbye to the hot sandbox. It was a bittersweet moment because we were anxious to get home, yet saddened to leave our comrades from other units in Iraq.

We returned home to Fort Bragg and it felt like a dream come true. We were ready to begin a new chapter in our lives. Let me ask you a question: Have you ever been away from your family more than nine months at a time? If so, you may already know how that can take an emotional toll on your life. If you've never been separated from your loved ones, it is indescribable with words. It is a constant mental duel between parts of your heart and brain. It was especially difficult for two reasons; one, you didn't know if you were going to return alive. Two, when you arrive back home, your mind is constantly bombarded by the continuous chatter of the deployment.

Imagine how soldiers felt when deboarding the 757 and seeing their family members after a year! This feeling of joy and exhilaration fills your heart. The feeling of gratitude overwhelms the human body yet the precious moments that were missed while away fighting a war will never be replaced.

As we gathered for our mandatory formation, our battalion chaplain asked everyone to bow his or her head for prayer. We had a moment of silence for our fallen comrades and the chaplain began to thank the Lord for our safe arrival and asked God to continue to graciously bless our lives. It was one of the most heartfelt prayers I had ever heard. At the end of his prayer there was a thunderous "Amen" from the soldiers and family members. We all could finally heave a sigh of relief because we were out of the danger zone.

The family members hugged, kissed, and cried as they saw their soldier come home. It was a phenomenal experience. Everyone was glad, happy, and proud. All that was heard were laughter and sniffles from the tears of joy. The Family Support Group did an amazing job coordinating the homecoming event. Banners were everywhere. The welcoming committee planned the event so well it were as if the POTUS stepped off the plane and had a welcome home ceremony. This was a full-blown party, a mature and responsible one that is. We enjoyed each other's company, and reminisced on happy moments both before leaving for Iraq and when we were in Iraq. The Army band played the most amazing songs to celebrate the arrival. Balloons were released into the air, and the excitement was contagious. The expressions of joy could be felt with your hands. There were tears, laughter, and emotions soaring in the atmosphere. It was ecstatic, to say the least. It felt as if God were there watching over us, and smiling and celebrating with us. News reporters were there to cover the battalion's victory and the redeployment process. There was so much excitement in the air, it made it difficult for the reporter to hear himself over the welcoming crowd. This was absolutely one of the best times while serving in the military. Returning home from combat to bond with family, friends, and loved ones made the year's deployment worthwhile. Additionally, it made one very appreciative of the small things most humans take for granted. Some soldiers were so grateful to arrive safely, they literally kissed the ground once they departed from the flight. It was truly an experience, and I would not trade anything for my journey in life.

Key Insight

As I served in the United States Army, I learned many valuable lessons. One of the most important lessons I learned was to value my time. Time is one of the most precious commodities we have. We should cherish and invest our time with the ones we love and choose our time wisely.

CHAPTER 11

The Battle Is Over...
Life After Retirement

"Life begins at retirement" -Author Unknown

The battle is over... the soldiers returned home safely... now what? Will they remain in the military and reenlist for another assignment? Could there be another deployment looming over our battalion's head causing soldiers to feel the anxiety and stresses of redeploying? These were the dreadful thoughts most soldiers silently contemplated while attempting to enjoy their time with the family.

Some soldiers ETS'd, while others retired from the military. ETS literally means separation from the military because of the Expiration of Term of Service. When exiting the military, a veteran will receive a form called a DD Form 214. This important document indicates the total length of service and whether he or she served honorably. This is one of the most crucial forms needed when departing from the military. The form basically tells your life story while on active duty. It accurately depicts your name, SSN, branch of service, highest rank achieved, date of birth, last duty assignment, primary specialty (your job), decorations, medals and awards, and who you list as your nearest relative. The last but most important item on the DD Form 214 is block 24. This block describes your character of service, and trust me when I tell you it should be marked "Honorable." When you retire or separate from the military, most employers will ask for a copy of your "214." This gives the employer some additional information about your knowledge, skills, and abilities. It is a good indicator of your reliability, trustworthiness, and marketability.

Once retired from the military, there were many necessary decisions to make. As an Apache pilot, my mission was to help ground forces make it home safely. My philosophies and goals in life did not change because I retired from the military. I still had a desire to assist others. In fact, my desire to help others increased even more because giving back to the community is my purpose in life. One of the ways I chose to give back to the public sector was going back to a private university and completing yet another degree as a registered nurse.

The benefits of serving in the military are astonishing. If one happens to join the military, the possibilities are endless. If you joined while owing a debt to a college or university, the military often offers a debt repayment plan; however, you are obligated to serve the military a few additional years. There are sign-on bonuses, depending on the Military Occupational Specialty selected. After you exit the military, there are additional benefits for the service member and children. The government pays handsomely and generously to those who work in the military, but many who join do not enlist for the monetary benefits. I find it particularly important to serve your country when you can and are able to. The above statement is not a recruitment tactic.

However, I would be remiss if I did not mention the extraordinary advantages of serving your country. My family and I are reaping the benefits every week as we shop in the commissary, purchase items from any military installation, or visit any military hospital in the world.

When I arrived from the war in Iraq, I began to recall some of the gruesome events that happened. I wouldn't sleep and I would have night terrors. The frequency of nightmares and restless nights eventually led to a divorce after 14 years of marriage. We slept in separate rooms due to her fear of my nightmares. One of the reasons the divorce rate is extremely high for military personnel is the lack of knowledge spouses possess concerning PTSD. My ex-wife did not understand the intricate details of a post-war veteran and how to cope with the differences. Although it was a devastation, I thank God for allowing me to move forward with my life.

I developed a need for more adrenaline after coming back from the war zone. I always needed a steady supply of adrenaline, when it came to flying and searching for terrorists while in Iraq. Upon returning home, driving a car at high speeds didn't satisfy my rush. There was nothing like feeling the rush of energy that came with flying an Apache helicopter. I made the decision to join a motorcycle club and begin to ride motorcycles again. I would ride from city to city at high speeds seeking to satisfy my cravings. This temporarily gave me the adrenaline rush I needed, but I soon realized I needed something more.

One dreadful evening, I was involved in a serious accident. I overcorrected my motorcycle, causing my front tire to hit a curb thereby making myself and the cycle fly 80 feet onto the highway. I hit the cement and instantly lost consciousness. I woke up in an Emergency Room with a neck brace, broken arm, head concussion, and three broken fingers, among a plethora of other injuries.

I was thankful to be alive but also flustered, frustrated, and upset knowing I was incapable of lifting, writing, and completing the basic functions as a human. I had never been without the use of my extremities and it was an overwhelming experience, but I would adapt and adjust. Thankfully, all my injuries were temporary and after a few months I would be working fine and as if I were never in the accident. It was these difficult times that allowed me to focus on the goodness of the Lord and how He kept his loving arms around me even when I made terrible mistakes.

I managed to overcome the hurdles of the accident. I even became ambidextrous in order to keep studying. I decided that if I wanted to give back, after defending my country, I must take action and work towards my new goals in life. Those goals were in line with my philosophy of helping others to succeed. Although I was not defending my country in combat, I embarked on a second career that brought much satisfaction and a sense of purpose that eventually made the adrenaline rush subside. I discovered yet another purpose for my life and it brings much satisfaction.

I was determined to continue my education, so I applied to several colleges/universities. I completed all of my prerequisites for nursing school at a state college and prayed long and hard for my acceptance into a private university. One month later, I received an acceptance letter to Jacksonville University School of Nursing. I was excited to receive the acceptance letter, but I had a broken arm; how could I possibly make it through nursing school? The day of the interview, I had to wear my sling. I asked the nursing staff to ignore my current physical situation as I would be back to normal within a month or so.

Additionally, I told them why I wanted to become a registered nurse and that I would work harder than others. With determination in my voice and a glint of strength in my eyes, I won the interviewers over and in no time I was present in lectures and classes.

This time, my degree happened to be in the field of medicine. Medicine is somewhat similar to aviation in that it constantly evolves. New discoveries are constantly improving the patient quality of care and lifestyle. Like aviation, simulation plays an integral part in nursing.

A wonderful thing took place in my life prior to starting nursing school. I saw a beautiful woman leaving a Chinese restaurant. I observed her for a while before my instincts told me to talk to her. I went over and began to talk to her. After much talking I found out that she was a nurse. I talked to her about the nursing career and why she chose nursing as a profession. The talking was both for my education and a plan to get her digits. After a short while of talking I gathered the courage to ask for her number; she politely gave her cell number as I eagerly saved it in my contacts list on my phone.

I waited a while to call her because I did not want to appear too anxious, but you better believe I could not keep my mind from this woman. Her speech was soothing to my ears. She had a demeanor and personality like none other. She was a woman of virtue and I knew that from the moment we spoke. I finally mustered the courage to call her and she positively accepted. We went out for lunch that same day and she was enamored by my conversation. Trust me, I was on my best behavior!

We got to know each other and after two years of courting, I proposed and she graciously accepted. Cherica has not only been a wonderful wife, but a faithful friend who I trust wholeheartedly. She has been my equalizer for life; for that I am grateful. We both have the same mindset, and we care for each other deeply. Needless to say, the two have become one.

The nursing career has been another rewarding vocation in that it offers so many approaches to helping others. It gives me the opportunity to help those in need and now teach nursing students the importance of learning the fundamental skills as a nurse. There are no words that can express how it makes you feel when your life consists of helping others whether they are patients, veterans, loved ones, or students.

No matter how small something may seem, it can go a long way. Although I was *Stacked Against the Odds*, I continue to make improvements in my life. Thanks to the grace of God, long hours of work, and sacrifice, I have accomplished many of my goals. These are just a few of the circumstances and how I overcame them. Key Insight

One person I want to mention is Helen Keller, who also at one time was *Stacked Against the Odds*. She was born on June 27, 1880, in Tuscumbia, Alabama. This woman was hit by scarlet fever at the young and tender age of 19 months. She lost her ability to see and hear. One thing she had in her favor was a great mentor in her life by the name of Anne Sullivan. Anne's ability to teach Helen was remarkable. She, too, was stricken with visual impairments, and this caused her to be lacking in ordinary skills. With surgery, Anne was able to overcome her visual impairments and received valedictorian in her class at age 20. She later was hired to assist 7-year-old Helen Keller with her obstacles. Helen was able to overcome these obstacles with her mentor, Anne Sullivan, who was able to push her beyond her limits.

Helen accomplished so many things such as learning to speak, read, and write. She adapted so well that she even wrote an autobiography. She also wrote essays such as "The World I Live In," "Let Us Have Faith," and "The Open Door." She overcame her obstacles and even managed to do something extra. She was even listed as an author in her passport. She addressed the world in many occasions through her written words, and so many deaf and blind people and writers look up to her. Many Americans also see her as an inspiration because she overcame so many things that others would have given up on. She addressed the rise of fascism and World War I, and was a devoted socialist. She even advocated the right for women to vote. She had overcome her difficulties and constraints in order to be able to find her God-given purpose and fulfill it. She was an overall optimistic person. I am not saying that you have to be blind or deaf to achieve your goals and purpose. Just think of all the possibilities out there. Many people out there have it in such a difficult way yet they find a way to get over the cliff and continue on their path. Imagine how empowering it feels to know that if she had so many things against her and she succeeded, then you can as well. The battle is over... Let that sink in.

Afterword

Remember that I dedicate this book to YOU. This book was specifically written with you in mind, and I hope that you will heed my advice. It is crucial you keep your eyes on the ball and do not let others take it from you. Your dreams are like seeds, and when you put them in soil and water them with the sweat of your hard work, they will flourish and give fruit. Do not let anyone take your seeds from you.

No matter who walks in or out of your life, you must advance and finish what you start. Remember you are only as good as your word. I encourage you to get up and explore the world to fulfill your purpose and go anywhere necessary to accomplish your goal.

With all this said, I wish the best for you and I hope that everything you want will be fulfilled. Anything can happen and only you can determine your outcome.

About the Author

As a motivational speaker, author, pilot in command, and registered nurse, Anthony offers a vast amount of expertise and knowledge to his audience. He joined the military at the young age of 17 to pursue his dreams. After 23 years of service, he retired from the U.S. Army at the age of 40. His tours of duty include: Fort Jackson, South Carolina; Fort Rucker, Alabama; Fort Campbell, Kentucky; Fort Stewart, Georgia; Hunter Army Airfield, Savannah, Georgia; Fort Bragg, North Carolina; Fort Hood, Texas; Camp Humphreys, South Korea; and Baumholder, Germany. Additionally, he served two tours in Iraq; Operation Desert Shield/Desert Storm 1990–1991, and Operation Iraqi Freedom III 2005–2006.

He is happily married to his beautiful wife Cherica, and they reside in Jacksonville, Florida. He earned two bachelor's degrees, one from Columbia College, and one from Jacksonville University. He serves as a clinical lab instructor in nursing and is currently pursuing a master of science from Jacksonville University. He wishes to pursue his Ph.D. in the near future.

Anthony's awards for meritorious accomplishments include Two Air Medals, Combat

Aviation Badge, Senior Aviation Badge, Defense Service Medal, Air Assault Badge, Meritorious Service Medal, Joint Service Commendation Medal, Southwest Asia Service Medal w/ Bronze Service Star, Global War on Terrorism Service Medal, Kuwait Liberation Medal, and Joint Service Commendation Medals.

To contact the author/write:
Anthony Fisher Enterprises

P.O. Box 28676 Jacksonville, FL, 32226

Email: aefisher68@gmail.com

www.AnthonyFisherSpeaks.com

Glossary

Alternate Flight Aptitude Selection Test (AFAST)
Advanced Individual Training (AIT)
Chief Warrant Officer Three (CW3)
Improvised Explosive Device (IED)
Forward Operating Base (FOB)
Military Occupation Specialty (MOS)
Meritorious Service Medal (MSM)
Operation Iraqi Freedom (OIF)
Warrant Officer Candidate School (WOCS)
President of the United States (POTUS)
Remain Over Night (RON)